Homeless Culture and the Media

Homeless Culture and the Media

How the Media Educate Audiences
in their Portrayal of America's Homeless Culture

Jeremy Reynalds

CAMBRIA
PRESS

Youngstown, New York

This book has been registered with the Library of Congress.
Reynalds, Jeremy
        Homeless Culture and the Media / Jeremy Reynalds
        p.   cm.
        Includes bibliographical references
        ISBN: 0-9773567-1-X

Contents

Foreword

The news media in the United States are supposed to play an essential role in our democracy by helping us monitor the world around us, bringing us the stories that happen beyond the range of our own senses. Too often, however, the media are distracted from important stories by politicians, business people and others who are particularly adept at gaining the attention of the media.

The homeless people in our society are not very good at getting news coverage. They end up on the front pages of newspapers and on newscasts most often when they are involved in a violent crime, either as criminals or as victims. One result is that most Americans understand very little about the homeless and the condition of being homeless.

Indeed, too many of us look at the homeless as being just unlucky. Some of us can imagine ourselves homeless if we were to miss a couple of paychecks. As a result, many of us tend to avert our gaze when we encounter the homeless on the street or we dig up a small handout to assuage our conscience. But for most people who are homeless, the problems are deeper than a missed paycheck or a bit of bad luck. Many people among the homeless are mentally ill or they abuse drugs and alcohol. And some are vicious predators who prey on other homeless people. A token handout given on a street corner will provide precious little real help to any of these homeless people. The needs are much deeper.

Few people in the United States understand the homeless and the condition of being homeless better than Dr. Jeremy Reynalds. Once homeless himself, Dr. Reynalds for years has run a faith-based homeless shelter that he founded to provide real help to homeless people who are serious about getting back into mainstream society. Dr. Reynalds literally lives with the homeless, day in and day out, as he runs his shelter and lives on the grounds of the shelter. Now Dr. Reynalds has examined the homeless and the media and their interaction very carefully in a new academic study.

Dr. Reynalds' study of a huge sample of news stories from major media across the country demonstrates that news media coverage of the issue of homelessness is largely superficial, hardly the kind of coverage that will help the average American understand the plight of the homeless.

But Dr. Reynalds' study of print and broadcast journalists suggests they are not likely to spend much time or effort to improve their coverage of the homeless.

Yet his talks with the homeless show they expect more from the media and are deeply critical of the shallow coverage the news media give them and their plight.

Dr. Reynalds' study broadens our understanding of the troubles of the homeless and helps us see what we don't know. Reading his study gives us new understanding of the beggar on the street corner and the stumbling drunk looking for shelter in an alley or under a bridge. It tells us about a piece of America few of us understand or worry very much about.

– Bob M. Gassaway, Ph.D.
Associate Professor
Department of Communication and Journalism
University of New Mexico

Acknowledgements

I wish to extend my sincere thanks to Dr. Don Douglas of Biola University's School of Intercultural Studies. He was a great encouragement to me over the years I spent commuting between Albuquerque, N.M. and Biola University in Los Angeles for classes for my Ph.D. His wisdom contributed greatly to this book.

In addition, I want to thank my long-time academic mentor, Dr. Bob Gassaway of the University of New Mexico's Communication and Journalism Department. Dr. Bob's influence in this book has been profound and is gratefully acknowledged. He was also with me throughout the entire length of my academic journey, and I was honored to have him as a member of my Ph.D. committee. Dr. Bob taught the very first class which I took as an undergraduate student at the University of New Mexico; his copy editing class made an indelible impression upon me; he was my committee chair for my master's thesis, and I am profoundly grateful for his ongoing friendship and encouragement.

I also want to thank my assistant, Roseann Vona Page, for her unparalleled expertise as she read through this manuscript. It was thanks to her skills and ongoing encouragement that you have the book you are holding in your hands today. In addition to being a valuable colleague, Roseann has become my closest confidant and dearest friend, helping me navigate through an intensely difficult personal situation during the past year. Roseann, I will be forever grateful that the Lord brought you into my life.

In addition, I want to thank Dr. Sue Alice Erickson, who provided extensive copy editing assistance, Carolyn Abbott, who transcribed all of the interviews, and my readers Travis Gallegos and Dee Robertson. Dee also interviewed those individuals staying at Joy Junction.

Homeless Culture and the Media

1

Background and Significance of the Study

Introduction

This qualitative study offers multiple perspectives regarding the news media's coverage of homeless people. Throughout, I hope to better inform you about the cultural phenomenon known as "homelessness."

I look at a sample of homeless people; their characterization and description of themselves in the news media; journalists' responses to those observations, and a sample of stories from the print and television news media that provide the dominant culture with accounts of the homeless and homelessness. The role of the media in depicting the homeless is a key issue here.

As cognitive psychologist Richard Jackson Harris asserts, the mass media are "a 'magic window' through which we view the world, but also the 'door' through which ideas enter our minds" (2004, p. 3). The metaphor of the window is especially useful in understanding how ordinary citizens learn about homeless people and the state of being homeless. Most Americans have no personal familiarity with homeless people; therefore they depend heavily on depictions of the homeless in the news media. Thus ordinary citizens learn about the homeless and homelessness from the media, just as they learn about political candidates, the functioning of government and most other aspects of society beyond the range of the individual citizen's senses.

Media researchers Rivers, Schramm and Christians noted: "Undoubtedly, the most important role of the media is to feed the ground – to deposit layers of information, day by day, hour by hour, so that a base is laid for the knowledge on which we walk. Compared with the occasional great and dramatic changes we can attribute to the media, this slow, continuing, never-ending effect is immensely more powerful and significant" (1980, p. 28–9).

I deal with three key areas of focus: (1) an analysis of how the mass media informally educate their audiences about the culture of homelessness in the United States through their descriptions and presentations of homeless people; (2) the results of a series of interviews with a theoretical sample of homeless people that explores how they describe themselves and how they perceive their portrayal by the mass media; and (3) the results of a series of interviews with a theoretical sample of Albuquerque, New Mexico-based print and broadcast journalists in which the journalists were asked to respond to the major concerns raised by the homeless interviewed for this project about the media's portrayal of homelessness.

I have identified two major ways that the general public learns about homeless people: (1) through their portrayal in the print and broadcast mass media; (2) by the public's own direct observations as the homeless appear in their local communities, perhaps while soliciting handouts or traveling about within local communities. This latter approach – directly observing the homeless – is the method least likely to provide useful information because many members of the general public, and especially those in moderate- to high-income brackets, may go for days, or even weeks, without seeing a homeless person. When they do see them, it is commonly only a glimpse of the person from the window of a passing automobile. Thus, media portrayals are the primary sources of information about the homeless for most Americans. I will:

- analyze how local and national mass broadcast and print media portray the homeless
- report on the responses of a theoretical sample of homeless people who were asked how they perceive themselves, how they feel they are portrayed in the mass media, and how they believe they are understood by the general public
- report on the responses of a theoretical sample of journalists based in Albuquerque, New Mexico, who were asked to respond to the major concerns raised by the homeless interviewed for this project regarding the media's portrayal of homelessness.

Outline

Chapter One establishes the purpose of the research, the statement of the problem, the hypothesis and the methods to be used. Chapter Two provides a review of the relevant literature dealing with this issue. Chapter Three provides an overview of the methodology used. Chapter Four provides data from the interviews of homeless people and media professionals in

Albuquerque, New Mexico. Chapter Five provides an analytical overview of interviews conducted with the homeless and some members of the media in Albuquerque, New Mexico. Chapter Six looks at the theories through which the findings of this research project are analyzed. Chapter Seven analyzes portrayals of the homeless in the mass media. Chapter Eight provides final conclusions from the results of the research, presents recommendations and provides opportunities for further study.

Most people do not have face-to-face encounters with the homeless; in fact, many of us try to avoid such encounters. People generally gain their knowledge and form their opinions regarding the homeless from their own exposure to news stories in the media, i.e., what they have read in the newspapers or heard on radio or television. While such knowledge and opinion may be distorted due to inaccuracies or distortions in the reporting (Hartman & Husband, 1974), people are, nonetheless, generally willing to express their opinions on the issue of homelessness because they believe the information they have received from the media.

In fact, people think they are being educated about what is going on in the world because they view television and read newspapers. However, many national television news broadcasts and other national media portray the homeless as ordinary people whose problems can be "fixed" by a meal and some overnight shelter. This portrayal is at odds with the experiences of many homeless service providers.

Donors from among the general public to ministries and other service providers to the homeless respond generously to appeals that emphasize the need for food and overnight shelter. They do not respond well to appeals that emphasize the need to fund rehabilitative programs, which most homeless services providers understand are an integral part of seeing alcohol and drug dependent homeless people reintegrated into mainstream community life.

General Statement of the Issue or Problem

I examine the relationship of national print and electronic media in their limited and oftentimes misleading portrayal of the homeless.

The book comprises, in part, a content analysis of both print and electronic media stories, in order to determine exactly what picture the national media are presenting to the public.

The analysis will identify whether or not the media are, intentionally or inadvertently, promoting a picture of the homeless as otherwise ordinary people whose problems can be "fixed" by a meal and some overnight shelter.

Project Overview

The research methods used were interviewing and analysis of the interview narrative. While content analysis was used, it was not employed as a research method, but as a technique used to quantify the characteristics of the media reports on homelessness and the homeless as found. This permitted a summarization of the media reports and provides an analytic approach to the media reports which constitute the data in this portion of the study (Appendix A).

Forty-one (41) people were interviewed for the main project. These comprised a national homeless advocate, a writer nationally acclaimed for his writings on poverty and America's changing approach over the years to dealing with poverty, an international journalist who heads a Christian news service, two print reporters, five broadcast journalists and thirty-one (31) homeless individuals. The interviews were conducted primarily in February and March 2004. The questions asked of the homeless are presented in Appendix B; their interviews appear in Appendix C.

An ethnographic study (Appendix D) was used for a pilot study conducted in February and March of 2002. The pilot study is an important part of this research. It is a snapshot of who the homeless actually are, as opposed to who the media claim they are.

In addition to the ethnographic observation, 12 individuals were interviewed for the pilot study (Appendix E).

Shelter activity logs (included in Appendix F) are also an important part of this research because they provide an additional picture that shows who the homeless actually are, as opposed to who they are portrayed to be. Briefly put, the activity logs often, but not always, are negative. These provide snapshots of life, reflecting the daily activities of homeless people housed at Joy Junction. As part of their duties, Joy Junction personnel and program participants record every incident that they feel needs to be brought to the attention of or addressed by shelter managers. These reports include summaries of events in which the police came onto the Joy Junction property, new guests arrived seeking housing, allegations of drug or alcohol use, which are prohibited, and disagreements among guests at the shelter. As a result, the logs often reflect the outbreak of hostilities and anger among guests of the shelter. The logs also provide descriptions of routine issues that need to be taken care of, such as putting locks on trucks, the need to check a dumpster, and the need for a driver to change among the vans used to transport residents to the shelter.

For example, as contained in Appendix F, one individual commenting on an incident wrote in the log, "Patrick came in drunk, and this was his third time on the alcohol list. Driver took him to People for Jesus church on 5600 Central S.W."

Another individual wrote in the log, "Rita called in, as Lois and the van driver did not pick her up as she is on the not welcome list."

A comment in the log from another individual read, "There was a confrontation between overnighters Doug and Jessie. They were yelling in each other's faces, slapping and pushing; the two were separated and told to stay away from each other. This is the second confrontation in the past week."

The respondents selected were a theoretical sample. Those residents interviewed at Joy Junction were members of the shelter's Life Skills Program. The homeless people I interviewed were not staying at Joy Junction. They had responded to a sign-up sheet placed at three Albuquerque agencies by a marginally "homed" individual who coordinated this interview section of the project. The homeless respondents were compensated $10 and the coordinator was compensated $50.

Media personnel interviewed were those with whom I had enough of an ongoing relationship, due to my work at Joy Junction, to contact. The questions asked of the media personnel arose as a result of the responses from the homeless interviewed. There was no written list of questions. The media interview sessions were much more unstructured.

Question Form

I attempt to answer the question, "Do print and electronic media, as well as homeless service providers, present a misleading picture of America's homeless to the public?"

Education and Culture

It is important to remember that homelessness is a subculture. As John Doughty wrote in his paper (1995) "Anomie and Homelessness: An Ethnography of Rural Nomads," "Homelessness, like anomie, has a cultural definition ... Robert Merton saw anomie as a difference in the goals of society and some individuals and in the difference in the way society and some individuals achieved those goals" (Hilbert, 1989, p. 47).

Here is additional evidence that the homeless constitute a subculture in the larger American culture:

The homeless often are ostracized from conventional society because of their lifestyles; the lifestyle of homelessness may be chosen in some instances, but in other instances it seems forced on some people who must claim that lifestyle in order to obtain resources offered only to the homeless. Many homeless people lack the resources to keep themselves and their clothes clean at all times, making them objectionable to many members of mainstream society, which constitutes the dominant culture.

The homeless often beg for handouts, putting them at odds with mainstream society where the Puritan work ethic allegedly still is valued.

The homeless often consume alcoholic beverages and illegal and illicit drugs to excess, causing them to commonly present themselves in public view in an intoxicated state, which is objectionable to many members of the dominant culture and often constitutes a violation of the laws passed by the dominant culture.

Homeless people commonly associate with other homeless people with whom they share information about resources for food, housing, medical care and other needs.

The face-to-face interaction of the homeless helps them build a common knowledge of resources available to them and encourages the development of a specialized vocabulary and syntax that can be used to describe, typify and talk about resources available to the homeless.

A foundational premise of this work is that the media educate—albeit in an informal fashion. As a writer commented in an article on the website of the Center for the Integration of Research, Teaching and Learning, "Informal education takes place in the information channels that become the principal avenues for learning ... once formal schooling is completed. These channels include: mass media, the World Wide Web, museums and public talks."

Research Statements

The national media and some homeless service providers often present a misleading picture of America's homeless as otherwise ordinary people whose problems can be "fixed" by a meal and some overnight shelter. This understanding was fostered by my analysis of the print and broadcast media narrative.

The understanding that led to this hypothesis was also reinforced by the limited amount of literature available on how the media portray the homeless. While that is dealt with in the review of the literature, this brief comment explains the hypothesis.

A study by the nonpartisan Center for Media and Public Affairs reported finding an advocacy-type approach by the media to the homeless, one that suggested the need for government assistance to an aggrieved group. Ongoing private sector initiatives were rarely observed. "In addition, while presenting the homeless in a sympathetic light, the media distorted their social characteristics, in ways that understate the difficulty in addressing their needs" (Buck & Toro, 2002, p. 3).

Donors to ministries and other providers for the homeless prefer to think of the homeless as being just like them, so presenting a more accurate picture of the homeless as drunks, alcoholics and schizophrenics who nonetheless still need help, would severely diminish funding for the many ministries that serve the homeless.

There is nothing in the academic literature that provides a clear indication concerning what one might expect to find from this research. However, observation from my ministry, as well as other ministries and providers across the United States, appears to indicate that the thesis statements presented above will be proven.

Definition of Significant Terms

The following terms are used throughout the book, and the definitions given here are used to clarify those terms.

> *Homelessness*: People with "no fixed abode or nighttime shelter other than that provided by a private or public agency" (Caton, 1990, p. 20).

> *Informal education*: The lifelong process by which every person acquires and accumulates knowledge, skills, attitudes and insight from daily experiences and exposure to the environment – at home; at work; at play; from the example and attitude of family and friends; from travel, reading newspapers and books; or by listening to radio or viewing films or television. Generally, informal education is unorganized and often unsystematic; yet it accounts for the great bulk of any person's total lifetime learning, including the education of even a highly "schooled" person (Coombs & Ahmed, 1974, p. 8).

> *Non-formal education*: "Any organized activity with educational purposes carried on *outside* the highly structured framework of formal education systems as they exist today" (Coombs & Ahmed, 1974, p. 233). Non-formal education has also been described as: "Any organized, systematic, educational activity carried on outside the framework of the formal system to provide selected types of learning to particular subgroups in the population, adults as well as children" (Coombs & Ahmed, 1974, p. 8).

> *Formal education*: "The highly institutionalized, chronologically graded and hierarchically structured 'education system' spanning lower primary school and the upper reaches of the university" (Coombs & Ahmed, 1974, p. 8).

Entertainment-education (defined for the purposes of this study as a derivative of informal education): "The process of purposely designing and implementing a media message both to entertain and educate, in order to increase audience members' knowledge about an educational issue, create favorable attitudes, and change overt behavior. Entertainment-education seeks to capitalize on the appeal of popular media to show individuals how they can live safer, happier lives" (Piotrow et al., 1997; Piotrow, Meyer & Zulu, 1992; Singhal & Brown, 1996 – as cited in Singhal & Rogers 1999, p. 9).

Agenda-setting: Is defined for the purposes of this research as the importance of an issue on the mass media agenda.

Researcher Biases and Limitations of the Study

As well as being the author of this book, I have been in ministry to the homeless for more than 20 years and could thus be considered an insider. This fact may cause some people to question the credibility of the research. However, I compensated for this in three ways: 1) hiring two people to read the broadcast transcripts and the newspaper articles; 2) hiring a person to interview the homeless people staying at Joy Junction (this person was also one of the readers for media articles); 3) hiring a person who is marginally homed to aid me in identifying a sample of homeless people who were receiving services from three additional area agencies.

In addition, to mitigate an inherent bias the homeless individuals interviewed went beyond Joy Junction. I interviewed homeless people who were being assisted by three other Albuquerque, New Mexico-based agencies as described elsewhere.

Some of the material analyzed will not be random, but will be more of a theoretical sample. This means it would be inappropriate to infer the results of this research to all ministries to the homeless. In this study, the term "theoretical sample" is used in the sense originally described in Glaser and Strauss (1967) and subsequently in Glaser and Corbin (1998). Glaser and Corbin (1998, p. 73) describe this concept this way: "Sampling on the basis of emerging concepts, with the aim being to explore the dimensional range or varied conditions along which the properties of concepts vary." For this study, I attempted to meet this expectation by seeking out and interviewing people who understood the phenomena under study and who might be able to provide their applied insights.

2

Review of Relevant Literature

Introduction

There is very little in the academic literature regarding how the media portray homeless people. This section presents: 1) some of the major literature that deals with the informal educational function of the media; 2) studies dealing with the entertainment and education function of the media; 3) the literature that deals with the few studies that show how the media have portrayed the homeless. I conclude with 4) a review of the literature that looks at the poor from a Biblical perspective.

The Informal Educational Function of the Media

Using a historical and structural perspective, social communication studies researcher Enrique SANCHEZ-RUIZ' research (1983) analyzed the early days of television in Mexico in order to accurately assess "TV's predominantly commercial character and what have been the relationships of the medium with the process of economic development and with the State" (Sanchez-Ruiz, 1983, pp. 2–3).

After reviewing a large body of literature, Sanchez-Ruiz concluded that television and other commercial means of mass communication were powerful methods of informal education with much influence and potential influence on society (Sanchez-Ruiz, 1983, p. 1). He called television a "parallel school" (an equivalent to the education gained in a formal educational setting), even though he acknowledged that it is not socially regarded as such (p. 1).

Bearing in mind that TV is, as Sanchez-Ruiz put it, "a pervasive formal educator" (p. 3), he investigated the historical and structural sources of the "school's" curriculum. Or to put it another way, he wrote that "after determining what historical actors, forces and tendencies" (p. 3) were involved, he set out to explain:

1. Who had actually been the 'informal educators,' that is, what individuals, groups or classes have had control of the medium;
2. Who had benefited from the development and expansion of TV in

Mexico, and how those who have benefited from TV's presence and commercial nature are related with the groups and classes that have controlled and benefited from the development process in general;

3. What had been the social functioning of the medium, including what main functions television has fulfilled in Mexico's development process. (p. 3)

As a result of his research, Sanchez-Ruiz found that television in Mexico had drastically increased its influence. However, "at the same time, its influence has been increasingly concentrated in a few hands, in a process of monopolization that has culminated in its present structure: the State and a private corporation, Televisa, hold a duopoly over the pervasive informal education vehicle that ... is television" (p. 383).

The objective of education researchers Philip COOMBS and Manzoor AHMED was "to develop – on the basis of examining past experience, present evidence and any fresh ideas – improved information, analytical methods and practical guidelines that would be useful to those actually involved in planning, implementing and evaluating programs of non-formal education geared to rural development" (Coombs & Ahmed, 1974, p. 4).

These researchers hoped that their work would help the "planners and policymakers who are concerned with improving the conditions of life in the vast rural areas of the world's poorest countries" (p. 3) more clearly realize the outcomes of the choices with which they were faced (p. 4). As an integral part of their study, these authors assessed what they concluded were some basic educational needs for effective rural development. Those needs were: general or basic education, family improvement education, community improvement education and occupational education (p. 15).

The authors defined general education as formal education, basically the type of education expected to be achieved by primary and secondary schools. They considered "family improvement education" to be "designed primarily to impart knowledge, skills and attitudes, useful in improving the quality of family life on such subjects as health and nutrition, homemaking and child care, home repairs and improvements, family planning ..." (p. 15). The authors defined "community improvement education" as that which is "designed to strengthen local and national institutions and processes through instruction in such matters as local and national government, cooperatives, community projects ..." (p. 15). Finally, the researchers described "community education" as "designed to develop particular knowledge and skills associated with various economic activities and useful in making a living" (p. 15).

During the course of their work, Coombs & Ahmed (1974) realized that it was important to ascertain the nature of rural development and non-formal education. They wrote, "The literature proved of little help on these questions and thus we were forced to improvise some questions of our own. The problem is not simply to devise a dictionary definition; it was the profoundly more difficult task of trying to discover the real nature of non-formal education and of rural development and to understand the relationship between the two" (p. 232).

From their study, Coombs and Ahmed concluded that, when properly administered, non-formal education "is an indispensable and potent instrument of rural development" (p. 235).They also found that, with the right circumstances, "even the poorest of countries ... should be able to mobilize the resources and human energies for a considerable expansion of non-formal education in rural areas" (p. 235).

Finally, they concluded that developing countries will make more progress in non-formal education if they receive help from other countries. "There is no shortage of ways for external agencies to assist strategically, but to do so with greater effect they will be required to alter considerably their past policies, doctrines and modes of operation" (p. 235).

In his 1986 study, author and Latin America researcher Thomas LA BELLE reviewed the main trends of the 1970s and 1980s in non-formal education programs among the adult poor of Latin America and the Caribbean. He also dealt with the overall concept of adult education, looked at some programs from the vantage point of change and strategy, and questioned "the viability of such efforts to promote the well being of the poor" (La Belle, 1986, p. vi). In addition, La Belle examined "the dynamics of project control and implementation," along with their "ideological underpinnings," to successfully ascertain the various ways in which "programs contribute to the achievement of project and organizational goals as well as to the social and economic enhancement of project participants" (p. vi).

As part of his research, La Belle also examined the political and economic climate of the region he was studying in order to help his readers to understand the connection between non-formal education and ideology and the different models of development.

La Belle continued by dealing with the theoretical and conceptual issues that undergird non-formal education and social change. Next, he dealt with ideology, development and human capital programs and with issues such as popular education and revolutionary guerrilla warfare. He concluded his study with a summary of the difference between programmatic rhetoric and reality (pp. x–xi). From his research findings, La Belle noted that:

> If non-formal education programs have long-term, cumulative benefits they are likely to rest with the inherent contradiction noted in both formal and non-formal education. That is, while programs either perpetuate or are at the mercy of forces that maintain the status quo, they also might simultaneously promote the questioning of the existing social order. Whether that in turn will lead to some action is questionable, given outsider control operating is essentially an extension of structural constraints. Yet those who seek reform through these activities must find a way to retain optimism … Such is the never-ending credence that those who seek change place in education. (p. 265)

In assessing non-formal education in Ghana, editors KINSEY and BING presented both a description and an analysis of non-formal educational activities that were undertaken in Ghana during 1976 and 1977 (Kinsey & Bing, 1978, p. 3). According to the editors, the purpose of the project was to "share the ideas, problems and learning that emerged from this experience with those who are concerned with the improvement of rural non-formal education programs as well as the development of more effective collaborative relationships between American universities and such field programs" (p. 3).

Researchers were attempting to provide expert assistance in the theory of non-formal education theory and practice in areas of materials development, delivery systems, training and research. They emphasized the creation of a development process for non-formal education "which could be applied in different localities, rather than attempt to transfer specific techniques and materials" (p. 2–3).

They identified "a network of human and material resources ... which encourages programs for the promotion of skills and knowledge in such areas as family health and nutrition, agricultural productivity, literacy and numeracy and the development of community and cooperative organization" (p. 2).

Participating organizations in the project were the University of Massachusetts' Center for International Education, the University of Ghana's Institute of Adult Education, and The People's Education Association of Ghana (p. 2).

Kinsey and Bing reported that the early project development was most successful "in the numerous examples of personal collaboration around tasks of common concern, in the creation of awareness of new program ideas and preliminary skills in applying them, and in the sense of movement and the possibility of change that resulted." In addition, following the completion of the project in December 1977, the researchers reported that there were several program developments encouraged by the project, a number of which (at the time of writing) "are exceeding initial expectations."

They concluded by commenting that organizations, like individuals, work toward independence and the "fulfillment of their capabilities. To the extent that this cross-national project has contributed to these ends for each of the collaborating groups, it can be deemed a success" (as cited in Kinsey & Bing, 1978, pp. 201–203).

In his book *Learning in Social Action: A Contribution to Understanding Informal Education*, adult education researcher Griff FOLEY argued that those involved in adult education need to be aware of the "incidental" learning that occurs when people involve themselves in political activity, social struggles and volunteer organizations (Foley, 1999).

To develop his argument, Foley used case studies from various countries coping with diverse political, environmental and other challenges. "He shows how involvement in social action can help people to unlearn dominant, oppressive discourses and learn instead oppositional, liberatory ones. He relates these processes of informal learning in contested contexts to current thinking and practice in adult education and points the way to a more radical agenda." (Foley, 1999).

Foley used three dimensions to develop his theoretical framework and a "broad conception" of education and learning. He looked at the "struggle" between education and learning, as well as "an analytical framework which enables connections to be made between learning and education on the one hand and analysis of political economy, micro-politics, ideologies and discourses on the other." Foley's entire premise is based upon his perceived "need" to "break out of the strait-jacket that identifies adult education and learning with institutionalized provision and course-taking" (p. 6).

According to Foley, his major interest was how people learn in what he called "emancipatory struggle. Because I look for them, I see such struggles and learning everywhere, not only where one might expect to find them, in popular movements and social action, but also in workplaces (including educational institutions) and families" (p. 11).

Throughout his book, Foley argued that popular struggles and movements have a little-studied educative element, "which when examined yields insights into the dynamics and effects of social learning activity. Foley concluded by stating that understanding what has been learned in these struggles, both past and present, is essential "to the development of a truly emancipatory education and politics in our time" (p. 143).

Entertainment-Education Theory and Media Agenda-setting

In her book, *Soap Operas for Social Change*, Heidi NARIMAN, the International Information Manager at Televisa, S.A. de C.V. in Mexico City, detailed the theoretical and empirical methodology that undergirds an entertainment-education campaign. She shows how this strategy actually worked out in Mexico. Overall, as the author points out in the preface, her work links "communication and behavioral theory as related to the actual design and production of a communication campaign" (Nariman, 1993, p. xv).

Nariman defined what an entertainment-education soap opera is, while defining its theoretical components and then described how to successfully assemble an entertainment-education soap opera based upon initial research findings. Finally, she demonstrated how to build on Mexico's experience with entertainment-education soap operas.

Communication scholars Everett ROGERS' and Arvind SINGHAL's book, *Entertainment-Education: A Strategy for Social Change*, dealt with the theoretical underpinnings of entertainment-education, as they also examined potential ethical challenges posed by the strategy. These authors also provided an in-depth discussion of the enormously successful Peruvian soap opera *Simplemente Maria*, which was the unintentional precursor of entertainment-education.

Among other issues, Rogers and Singhal looked at an entertainment-education soap opera in India and at the effects of the strategy when applied to music and radio. They concluded their work by looking at the overall effects of entertainment-education and the lessons that have been learned about the strategy.

In the 1993 book *Serial Fiction in TV: The Latin American Telenovelas*, edited by Anamaria Fadul, several contributors analyzed Brazilian soap operas. After this assessment, contributors Everett Rogers, Arvind Singhal and William Brown discussed the strategy needed to produce a successful entertainment-education "telenovela." They pointed out (p. 151) that there are a number of things to do: decide on a central educational value everyone can agree on; find "an integrated multi disciplinary theoretical framework which, among other things, drew upon Bandura's (1977) social learning theory" (p. 151); and have access to a quality production system.

In her unpublished 1997 master's thesis, *The Impact of Social Learning Theory in an Entertainment-Education Radio Soap Opera*, communication researcher Krista ALFORD evaluated the effects of Albert Bandura's (1977) social learning theory in a Tanzanian entertainment-education soap opera, *Twende na Wakati*, or *Let's Go with the Times*. Alford tested three independent variables "for their differences and their correlations between family planning adoption as a result of listening to the soap opera" (Alford, 1997, p. v).

For each of the three independent variables she tested, Alford found that there were significant differences in the mean scores of nonadopters and adopters of family planning as a result of listening to *Twende na Wakati*. The same was true for the adopters of the three specific methods of contraception. However, she wrote, "there was not always a difference in the expected direction between the adopters of family planning methods other than the pill, injectables, or condoms versus adopters of the pill, injectables, or condoms respectively" (p. v).

In their book *Agenda-Setting* (1996), communication researchers James DEARING and Everett ROGERS deal with the multi-part theory of agenda-setting. In this particular instance they look at the importance of an issue on the mass media agenda. While the authors did not originate agenda-setting, they did popularize the concept. They identified three main components of the agenda-setting process, a) the media agenda, b) the public agenda, and c) the policy agenda. This book deals only with the media agenda in determining the way they portray the homeless.

Dearing and Rogers noted some generalizations about the agenda-setting process. They include that: a) during different time frames different media place varying degrees of importance on certain issues; b) the events occurring in the world (also known as real world indicators) are not terribly important in determining the media agenda; c) the White House, the *New York Times* and "trigger events" such as the recent tsunami disaster play an important role in seeing an issue placed on the media agenda; d) the results of scientific research do not play an important role in the agenda-setting process; e) the position of an issue on the media agenda helps to determine the issue's relevance or otherwise on the public agenda (Dearing & Rogers, 1996, pp. 90–92).

Addressing why some issues are not resolved, Dearing and Rogers said, "Homelessness … seems to be an unsolvable problem in the United States … Some social problems persist despite human attempts to resolve them. These long-term problems are occasionally made into 'issues' through certain trigger devices and/or issue champions" (pp. 97–98).

The Media and the Homeless

A study by the Center for Media and Public Affairs (CMPA), which describes itself as "a non-partisan research and educational organization that conducts scientific studies of the news and entertainment media," analyzed all television network evening news and news magazine stories from November 1986 through February 1989 (Center for Media and Public Affairs, 1990, p. 2). It "examined all topics, sources, themes, and viewpoints presented in 103 stories (3 hours 31 minutes of airtime) on ABC, CBS, and NBC; and 26 often lengthy stories (621 column inches) in *Time, Newsweek,* and *US News & World Report*" (Center for Media and Public Affairs, 1990, p. 2).

The CMPA study reported finding an advocacy-type approach by the media to the homeless, one that suggested the need for government assistance to an aggrieved group. Ongoing private sector initiatives were rarely explored. "In addition, while presenting the homeless in a sympathetic light, the media distorted their social characteristics, in ways that understate the difficulty in addressing their needs."

Highlights found by CMPA researchers included the following: "Only 25% of homeless people presented were described as unemployed, only 7% as drug and alcohol users, and only 8% as mentally ill. In contrast, the U.S. Conference of Mayors say that 77% of the homeless are unemployed, 34% are substance abusers, and 25% are mentally ill" (p. 2).

> Three out of four sources (74 percent) presented believed it was the government's responsibility to solve the issue of homelessness. 22 percent were in favor of combined public-private initiatives, and only four percent looked at private charity as a resource. The answer most frequently given was that there needed to be more government funding. 100 percent of those who looked at the government's role thought the government needed to be more involved. Seventy-percent of the anecdotes and illustrations presented by the media dealt with problems and failures. Only 30 percent focused on success stories, including successful or promising local programs. There were no positive stories featured by NBC, Time, and Newsweek on attempts to help the homeless; and CBS only aired one. (p. 2)

The Center researchers found that

> the media portrayed the homeless as ordinary people victimized by social and economic forces and requiring governmental assistance to address their needs. Homelessness was presented as a major social problem to which the political system must be forced to respond with public funding. But the human face of homelessness, hence

the nature of the problem, seems quite different from the media's portrayal. (p. 2)

In their study titled, "The Homeless in U.S. Electronic Media," communication scholars and researchers Rebecca Lind and James DANOWSKI found that overall there has been very little coverage of the homeless in the electronic media (as cited in Min, 1999, p. 118).

They pointed out that while

the few studies there have been on media portrayal of homelessness present conflicting findings on whether the media attribute the root causes of homelessness to the individuals themselves or to external social factors and the extent to which the homeless are presented as stigmatized, the bulk of the research has determined that most media portrayals blame homelessness on the homeless and often depict the homeless as deviant. (p. 110)

For their own research, Lind and Danowski analyzed the portrayal of the homeless in U.S. electronic media by analyzing the transcripts of about 35,000 hours of television and radio content aired on ABC, CNN, PBS and NPR from May 1993 to January 1996. They covered a larger amount of text than any other researchers had ever attempted to do, as well as using "a more rigorous methodology than is typical of most content analysis" (p. 109).

Using a computer-aided analysis program, Lind & Danowski looked for stigmatization, attribution, individualization, compassion, programs/policies/ solutions, and seasonal markers in the media's portrayal of the homeless. Out of the almost 130 million words analyzed, the researchers found 3,134 references to the homeless – only 0.0024% of the total number of words analyzed. To put it another way, the word "homeless" only appeared once about every 45,000 words (p. 113).

The researchers concluded that the homeless were "extensively stigmatized" in news and information programs. They found that the homeless were commonly presented as mentally ill substance abusers, often involved in criminal behavior, and often in poor health and suffering from contagious diseases. "The stigmatized image of the homeless that the audience receives is not countered by an alternative image encouraging sympathy and support" (p. 118).

Lind & Danowski found that while the media did not really deal with the causes of homelessness, "the state of being homeless was significantly less frequently blamed on homeless individuals than it was on a combination of things such as unemployment, a lack of affordable housing, the economy and natural disasters. This finding indicates a fairly positive portrayal of the homeless" (p. 118).

In her study of news media coverage of the homeless, communication researcher Bernadette MCNULTY wrote that news stories construct five different images of homeless people and convey news about the issue of homelessness in such a way as to suggest that nothing can be done to address the problem. McNulty identified two communication models; a) one that promotes a call to social action; and b) one that suggests hopelessness or resignation. McNulty used the models to suggest that news organizations showed "four different levels of resignation with reference to their presentation of components that either promote social action or suggest hopelessness" (McNulty, 1992, p. 271).

McNulty's study analyzed national print and broadcast media coverage of the homeless between November 1986 and February 1989. Her analysis included 103 network television news stories from all three networks, plus 26 articles printed in the major news magazines (p. 20).

According to McNulty, the news constructs five basic images of the homeless. These images focus on "social actors, relationships, behaviors, conditions and causes of homelessness," in which the homeless appear as "institution avoiders," "mentally-ill individuals," "families and children," "runaway or abandoned teens," and "threatening villains" (p. vii). She found that a variety of factors such as journalistic commentary, visual techniques and the use of statistical information all played a significant part in establishing the credibility and authenticity of the news account. "Images portray unambiguous sets of victims and villains, emphasize individualistic problem causes and contribute to resignation about homelessness" (p. vii).

Using a structuralist narrative approach, then doctoral candidate I. WHANG (1993) looked at a sampling of the television news coverage of the homeless between 1985 and 1991. Whang found that during this period, there was a combined total of 358 news stories on the three major networks. Realizing that he would be unable to view that number of stories, Whang sampled 25 stories (Whang, 1993, p. 98).

Whang looked at the media's coverage of homelessness based upon his personal experience of television viewing. He commented that, as a long-time television viewer, he had been "addicted" to "television news or documentary programs in particular because they are 'commonsensically' believed to deliver 'reality' as it is (in) the most faithful way" (p. 26).

Whang said that as a result of this "addiction," he viewed many stories concerning the homeless over a number of years, concluding that television news coverage particularly focused on the homeless and on charitable services providing help to the homeless during the Christmas and Thanksgiving seasons. Whang asserted that this was not the "proper" way of dealing with the issue of homelessness, as it was not one that could be solved by seasonal charitable giving. "In retrospect, I was certain that the news coverage of the homeless around these religious holiday seasons must have given the networks a good chance to 'repeat' their routines by making moving melodramas out of some religious happenings in order to arouse sympathetic feelings among the viewers by prettifying them" (p. 26).

Whang then looked at whether television news narratives present the homeless as "the victims of social problems or problem makers" (p. 30). As an integral part of his study, Whang attempted to identify the narrative structures of television news programs as they related to story and discourse (p. 30).

In his analysis, Whang found a "patterned" use of a number of semiotic elements that included lighting, setting, camera work and the portrayal of the character's primary actions. Whang said that the "patterned" way of visual encoding resulted in two types of character representations: one a portrayal of the homeless as individuals and the other as a collective mass. He observed that, as a rule and compared with other characters, the homeless tended to be portrayed "not as autonomous individual 'persons,' but as a 'collective' group at the non-personal level." He noticed this in the fairly common network use of long-range shots for both groups of homeless, "whereas the medium-range shots were mostly reserved for those characters whose 'authoritative' positional qualities tended to be socially recognized, such as professional homeless advocates, doctors, lawyers and ministers" (p. 209).

Conversely, Whang suggested that the networks' use of a high camera angle more often for the homeless than for other characters suggested that the homeless were many times seen as "emotion-oriented" characters rather than "rationality-oriented" ones. He added that the homeless tended to be framed the least often in the best shots (p. 210). Even when there were close ups of the homeless, Whang said that there was still a different effect between the homeless and other individuals. He noted that in most cases, what was said by the professional characters sounded like it was merely delivering the general, public opinion and thus seemed to represent society in general, but "what we heard from the homeless characters tended to be confined within their personal emotional reactions to their own everyday experiences and hardships, that is, those 'immediate effects' of the fact of 'being homeless'" (p. 210).

Whang said that in contrast to the "embedded" character narrators, the reporters and anchors received the most favorable treatment as "framing" narrators and were

> filmed in the optimal presentation modes such as medium-distance, standard eye-level angle, facing-the-camera orientation, plain backing in the studio (the anchor in particular), good lighting and decent formal dress ... Their direct eye contact mode of address along with the optimal visual framing contributed to establishing their positional quality of intimacy, neutrality, objectivity, credibility and authoritativeness" (p. 210).

Whang pointed out that the impersonal and objective sound of the anchor's voices was supported by a voice-over narration and graphical presentation of related information. This helped to increase the "realistic" tone of the "news team's own account of the 'homelessness' phenomena" (p. 211).

Whang said that both the homeless and other "embedded" narrators seemed to be placed in positions that were not meaningful unless they were placed within a certain framework, whereas anchors and reporters were advantageously placed to control the overall narrative. Whang wrote, "Because of this advantage, it was possible for the anchor to define the topic and assign the reporter of the day to lead the ... narrative by presenting evidence of their thesis, reinforcing the pre-established definition of the homeless and wrapping up the story in accordance with a given framework" (p. 218).

Whang asserted that it really did not even matter what kinds of "embedded" characters were used in the news stories, because it was primarily the reporter's presentation (supplemented by the anchor) that played the major role in directing the flow of the story from beginning to end. "In short it might be argued that television news is a narrative of which the overall flow is dominated and controlled by the 'verbal' narration of the 'framing' narrators, to which the visual presentation tends to be subjected" (p. 218).

Communication professor Katherine KINNICK's dissertation looked at whether "pervasive" media news coverage of problems such as homelessness may result in "compassion fatigue" toward the problem being covered. Kinnick developed a telephone survey that measured compassion fatigue in relation to serious social problems such as homelessness, violent crime, AIDS and child abuse. Kinnick administered the questionnaire to a random sample of residents of the greater metropolitan Atlanta, Georgia, area. She focused her research on the "constructs of interest, emotional arousal, and information-seeking areas for each issue. Data analysis also examined associations between burnout and possible antecedent variables. In addition, the study identified cognitive, affective and behavioral manifestations of compassion fatigue."

Kinnick's analysis showed that 15% to 40% of the people she questioned reported feeling burned out, depending on the issue being covered. Thirty-three percent reported feeling burned out in relation to coverage of the homeless, 40% on violent crime, 33% on AIDS and almost 15% on child abuse. She noted that for each of the issues, "reports of burnout were associated with significantly lower levels of interest, emotional arousal and information-seeking. Desensitization was found to be a more common reaction to pervasive media coverage than emotional over arousal" (Kinnick, 1994).

Overall, Kinnick observed, her analysis indicated the existence of compassion fatigue as a "situational phenomenon rather than a personality trait." As such, this "support[s] the assertions of media observers that the nature of contemporary media coverage about social problems may contribute to emotional fatigue with these issues" (Kinnick, 1994).

Kinnick pointed out that her findings pose some serious implications for news organizations. Because of the way they cover the homeless and other social problems, the media run the chance of losing at least some of their audiences. She noted that while the media's coverage may initially attract attention and bring resources in dealing with these social service issues, "pervasive coverage which emphasizes problems without solutions may actually backfire and create a numbing of concern toward social problems and their victims." The results of her research should also provide cause for concern for social service organizations, as these results "provide evidence to contradict the commonly held assumption of 'the more media coverage, the better' for the amelioration of social problems" (p. 177).

In his 1996 study titled "Estimating the Homeless: Media Misrepresentation of an Urban Problem," Christopher HEWITT of the University of Maryland's Department of Sociology and Anthropology, examined the nationwide estimates that were made during the 1980s of the number of homeless nationwide (Hewitt, 1996).

He argued that the claims by certain advocacy groups of two to three million people being homeless on any given night were unjustified. Pointing to social scientific studies, Hewitt noted that the real number of homeless was somewhere between 300,000 and 500,000. He said that such a discrepancy in figures was a good test of the news media's ability to distinguish between real social science research and guesstimates (Hewitt, 1996).

According to Hewitt, an examination of American magazines and newspapers found that, as a group, the media were more likely to offer higher, rather than lower, estimates and that this only changed slightly over time. Hewitt said that the two factors that could explain this apparent inability to distinguish between good and bad estimates are a) media bias; and b) the way that the information is gathered (Hewitt, 1996).

Hewitt pointed out that the emergence of homelessness in the 1980s as a major urban problem could be attributed to media coverage and the resulting public concern. The *New York Times* was featuring an article on some aspect of homelessness almost every day by the end of that decade, and television news was broadcasting between 40 and 50 news stories annually. Public opinion polls from the same time period found that much of the public perceived that the problem was getting increasingly worse; that the federal government was not doing enough and should be doing more (as cited in Hewitt, 1996).

While social scientists began to pay an increasing amount of attention to the problem, asking what kind of people the homeless were and why they had become homeless, in order for the results of the social science to be effective, the results had to be disseminated and accepted. What type of media coverage was provided, Hewitt found constituted an important part of the political response to homelessness (Hewitt, 1996).

Hewitt's paper focused on reported estimates of the number of homeless persons by the media because the issue defines journalists' ability to make a determination regarding good and bad social science (Hewitt, 1996). Hewitt said that, while it may have initially appeared that the media were unable to distinguish good research from bad research, that might be too pessimistic an assessment, as in the end the media did report the actual research figures of social scientists more than the (inflated) estimates provided by some of the homeless advocates (Hewitt, 1996). However, Hewitt pointed out that the need to distinguish good research from bad research did illustrate the need for social scientists to take responsibility for disseminating their research to the media and denouncing any false scientific claims of their research (Hewitt, 1996).

In his paper "Re-covering the Homeless: Insights on the Joyce Brown Story," communication professor and researcher Jimmie REEVES related that toward the end of the Reagan era, a homeless person named Joyce Brown achieved media "fame" when the city of New York removed her from where she was "living" above a heating vent and involuntarily committed her to a psychiatric ward in a New York City hospital. Collaborating with colleague and communication researcher Richard Campbell, Reeves undertook an analysis of the news coverage of the Joyce Brown situation and found that "it provided a limited set of texts that addressed an expansive set of cultural, theoretical and interpretive issues" (as cited in Min, 1999, p. 45).

In the initial research, Reeves analyzed the differences and similarities between three network news packages aired in early November, 1987, that portrayed a struggle between the efforts of a program to help those who were unable to help themselves against the constitutionality or otherwise of involuntarily hospitalizing the homeless. Reeves' fellow researcher, Campbell, used comparative analysis to demonstrate how "'60 Minutes' subsequent rewriting of the 'Brown vs. Koch' segment embodied many of the narrative conventions and mythic tensions of the most celebrated and popular news magazine in the history of American television" (p. 45). The researchers argued that the news coverage "explored the limits of government, freedom, compassion, individualism and the boundaries of common sense itself" (p. 45).

In taking another look at the Joyce Brown story, Reeves treated the issue as "a significant movement in the flow of 246 television news reports broadcast between 1981 and 1988 that collectively gave expression to the Reagan-era 'homeless narrative'." In his analysis, Reeves stated that he looked at the 246 news stories under consideration as a sort of "grand mosaic" that shaped itself around the "economic instabilities, cultural conflicts and political rivalries of the day" (pp. 45–46).

Summing up his findings, Reeves wrote that the real meaning of Brown's story cannot be seen in isolation, but only as it relates to other conflicts and struggles in that time period. Reeves said that the whole Brown affair can be thought of as

> a kernel event within the larger social drama of the homeless narrative within the larger antagonisms of the politics of rich and poor in post-Florist America. By the end of the Reagan era, in part because of the Brown controversy, the homeless had been redefined in the network news as a 'danger to themselves and others' – as a policing problem, a personal problem, or a problem for private volunteer organizations – but not an economic problem. (p. 60)

Researchers have also looked at the way the Japanese media cover the problem of homelessness in Japan. In their paper "Japanese Furoosha (Bums) and Hoomuresu (Homeless) Living in the Shadow of Wealth" (1999), communication researchers Richiko IKEDA and Eric Mark KRAMER examined the media's coverage of homelessness in Japan as they related the "cleaning up" of the homeless from a Tokyo street by Tokyo government employees and police officers (Min, 1999, p. 197). The government had decided to build a moving walkway on that street and needed to remove the homeless.

Despite their resistance to the move, the homeless were summarily expelled. The Tokyo government's offer of a shelter was only good for slightly more than two months. Of the 200-plus people removed that day, only 43 wanted to make use of the shelter anyway (p. 197). The day after the removal, government officials announced that they would put steel bars between the pillars placed along the walkway to permanently prevent the homeless from returning (p. 197).

The researchers pointed out that Japan has suffered from an economic recession since 1991. While it is therefore quite unlikely that a typical worker would actually end up homeless, the high profile of the homeless, in combination with the fear caused by the recession and the mass media's reporting of the homeless "cleanup" mentioned above, have together made the existence of the homeless practically untenable (p. 197).

As thousands of smartly-dressed, salaried men and women pass by every day, the contrast between those who have a job and home and those who do not is profound. Since the recession, the presence of the homeless makes the recession even more disturbing to the armies of workers passing by. The homeless are a reminder of what could, no matter how remotely, happen to those who lose their place in the system (p. 197).

Ikeda and Kramer contended that the mass media "sensationally" suggest to their viewers how close they could be to ending up homeless in the near future. The media also describe situations, the researchers alleged, where the homeless have been treated like garbage (p. 198).

According to the researchers, the Japanese media did not attach much importance to two killings of the homeless and that, they pointed out, is problematic. "When and how the media reports an issue creates the perception of its import. According to the theories of agenda-setting and status conferral, if the media treat a case as trivial, it becomes a trivial case … If an incident is not perceived it does simply does not exist" (pp. 209–210).

Ikeda and Kramer discovered that while the 1983 killing of two "bums" attracted quite a lot of media attention which in turn, according to the researchers, generated much public outrage, a lack of media attention to the 1995 killings had the opposite effect. The researchers questioned whether this signified a decrease in interest or desensitization between 1983 and 1995 (pp. 209–210).

Pointing out that other factors were also at work, they stated that editors and producers responsible for the coverage of the 1995 killings of the homeless had concluded that the murders of homeless people would not be of much interest to the general viewer; they would not sell. The change from using the word "bum" to "homeless" may be of interest because after researching the two major Japanese newspapers, Ikeda and Cramer concluded that it could be traced to the mid-1990s. The researchers added that using the term homeless denotes the belief that anyone, regardless of their effort, can become homeless. While use of the word "bum" tended to imply that the person being described was lazy, "being homeless connotes a consequence of a systemic force beyond one's control" (pp. 210–212).

Their implication seemed to be that the media's change of terminology was just reflecting a societal change. As Ikeda and Kramer wrote,

> Economic disjunction is not well understood and is poorly explained in the press. Economic forces have a tendency to be mystified and mystifying. The economy is practically a magical phenomenon. We are all part of it. The fear that comes from lack of understanding and real or perceived consequences is felt as personal vulnerability and anxiety. The term homeless may reflect such anxiety in Japanese society. Being uncertain results in fear or anxiety. (pp. 209–210).

The Poor: A Biblical Perspective

In his book *God of the Empty Handed: Poverty, Power and the Kingdom of God* (1999), Jayakumar CHRISTIAN, national director of World Vision in India, explored the relationship of poverty and powerlessness, using an integrated approach of anthropology, sociology, politics and theology. Christian analyzed some secular development theories as well as evangelical, Dalit and liberation theologies and assessed some traditional historical responses to poverty. He also looked at the real meaning of powerlessness, described some of the many challenges facing the Christian church today, and provided an alternative response that he believed explores the concept of power according to the theology of the kingdom of God.

Christian said that people dealing with the poor need to be authentic and that their response to the poor must focus on persons and relationships. There needs to be more than just a planned programmatic response. Additionally, he suggested that an appropriate kingdom-based response must be "based on truth. An integral part of training grassroots practitioners will be enabling them to become a hermeneutical community that constantly shapes and reshapes its paradigms and models of mission."

Christian also suggested that a kingdom-based response in working with the poor will include an on-going battle with principalities and powers. He said that "practitioners" consequently need to embrace the role of the Holy Spirit in their on-going efforts (Christian, 1999, p. 221).

An appropriate response also means that those who work with the poor need to have a Biblical understanding of how God deals with the poor. It should identify those Biblical "patterns" in God's dealings with the poor. And "because the roots of poverty are entangled in a people's worldview and religious systems, grassroots practitioners need reequipping with skills to analyze the worldview of a people as a necessary part of poverty analysis" (p. 221).

Christian also postulated that poverty workers need to be both equipped and willing to address global issues while working with the poor in their local communities. He stated that this is not what usually occurs; instead the bulk of any work with the poor is usually focused at a micro versus a macro level. He contended that to be effectively addressed, poverty must be dealt with at the variety of levels at which it occurs: micro, macro, global and cosmic.

Christian concluded his proposed plan by saying that kingdom power should cause "ripples of transformation," as it "equips the poor to be agents of transformation and thus initiate movements," and that a kingdom-based response affirms that power belongs to the Lord. "That means that those people who deal with the poor on a grassroots level must live their lives in a manner that affirms this statement. There will be a positive consequence for doing that," he commented, continuing, "This will enable the poor to perceive the link between power as expressed in a kingdom-based response and dependence of the community of practitioners on Jesus Christ, to whom all power and glory belongs" (pp. 220–221).

In his book *Walking with the Poor* (1999), Bryant L. MYERS, vice-president of International Program Strategy for World Vision International, drew predominantly on two sets of ideas: 1) professor of mission and anthropology, Paul Hiebert's description of the Western worldview and its excluded middle, and 2) Jayakumar Christian's belief that poverty has a spiritual basis while being founded in non-working relationships.

Hiebert articulated the Western worldview in two separate and distinct realms: the material and the spiritual. The gap that exists between the two, he called "the excluded middle." Hiebert said those who regard things from a Western perspective assume that "the location of cause and effect is in the material world. In contrast, traditional cultures believe that the cause of things is located in the unseen world of spirits and gods. The absence of a 'middle' in the Western worldview infers that there is no way to make sense of or respond to the very important 'middle' of traditional cultures." Bryant noted that this framework had been very helpful to him when dealing with the work of development promoters "and their tool kit of technological inventions."

Christian suggested that a major result of poverty for the poor is a "marring" of their identity. This is caused by the "grind" of being poor, "as well as their being captive to the god-complexes of the non-poor." Writing about Christian, Myers said:

> It also mars the identity of the non-poor. They cannot play God and be who they are in God's sight. To Christian's proposal that transformation is the work of helping the poor recover their true identity as made in the image of God, I add the idea that vocation or calling is also part of true identity … The poor and the non-poor need God's redemptive help to recover their true identity as children of God made in God's image and their true vocation as productive stewards, given gifts by God to contribute to the well being of all. (Myers, 1999, p. xviii)

In his book *The Tragedy of American Compassion* (1992), journalist and professor Marvin OLASKY argued for a different approach. He showed that the social programs of the welfare state do not provide an answer for the problems of the poor, nor does money provide a way out.

American Institute Fellow Charles Murray pointed out in his preface to Olasky's book that descriptions of a so-called poverty-stricken "underclass" can be found from the beginnings of the writings of American sociology, and, in fact, go back to the early days of colonial America. However, the proportion of people who fit that description was extremely small; much smaller than now, when "poverty was so much closer to real destitution than 'poverty' as we know it today" (Olasky, 1992, p. xv).

Attempting to answer that question, Olasky contended that human needs used to be answered by other human beings with a non-compartmentalized response, as opposed to bureaucracies. "People didn't use to be so foolish as to think that providing food would cure anything except hunger, nor so shallow as to think that physical hunger was more important than the other human hungers, nor so blind as to ignore the interaction between the way that one helps and the effects of that help on the human spirit and human behavior" (p. xv).

In the World Vision publication titled *Working with the Poor: New Insights and Learnings from Development Practitioners*, a variety of grassroots development practitioners (poverty workers) answered the question, "How do Christian practitioners express authentically holistic transformational development?" According to the book's jacket notes, the continuing dilemma is a Western assumption that there are two separate and distinct realms: physical and spiritual, with the jacket writer suggesting that

> such a dichotomy leads to a belief among practitioners that restoring people's relationship with God has nothing to do with restoring just political, social and economic relationships among people. Even Christians often believe that God's redemptive work takes place in the spiritual realm, while the world is seemingly to be left to the devil. But the Bible never separates the physical from the spiritual – the rule of God permeates both. (Myers, 1999, p. xviii).

Contributors to the book reflected on a variety of issues. The topics included the meaning of poverty, the Bible and transformational development, community development and peace building and participatory learning and action.

As the research has shown to this point, there is very little in the literature dealing with how the media portray the homeless. A search of the EBSCO

Host Database on October 20, 2005 revealed that while there were only 82 articles containing both the terms "homeless and media," together, there were 8,214 articles containing the term "homeless" alone and 172,604 articles containing the term "media" alone.

From the available literature summarized in this chapter, this book uses primarily the entertainment-education theory popularized by Everett Rogers and the Biblical theory of Jayakumar Christian.

3
Research Methods

In order to understand how the media cover homeless people and the state of homelessness, I studied a sample drawn from 2,300 news stories reported by Fox News, CNN, CBS, ABC, NBC, the *New York Times*, the *Los Angeles Times* and the *Albuquerque Journal*. The text of the stories was obtained from the LexisNexis database, using the keyword "homeless" as a search term.

Each story selected for the sample was read and coded at the nominative level as a beginning point of content analysis. The following system of analysis was used. News stories in the sample were put into four categories. The coding system was quite simple:

A story was coded "0" if it contained the word 'homeless' but did not deal with the issue. For example: In a number of broadcast media stories, an anchor would say, "In our next segment we will be dealing with the homeless."

A story was coded as a "1" if there was only a peripheral mention of the homeless. For example, if a person arrested for shoplifting was identified only as a homeless person but no other information about the person's homeless state was provided, this was coded as a 1 because this mention of the person being homeless is merely a journalist's way of saying the person had no address, a common item of information in a news story. For example, one story coders encountered very often was about a homeless man who was hit by a car, flew up and was impaled in the windshield. The licensed practical nurse driving the car did not stop or render aid; she drove her car on home with the man partly inside the car and partly on the hood. The woman parked her car in her garage and allowed the man to die slowly over the next couple of days. News stories reported very little about the man and his background, except that he was homeless.

A story was coded as a "2" if the story dealt with the issue of homelessness. For example: The difficulties faced by the homeless in getting back on their feet again or a shortage of beds for the homeless in New York.

A story was coded as a "3" if it dealt with the homeless but not the issue of homelessness. This category usually dealt with crimes or acts committed by or against the homeless, such as the Elizabeth Smart kidnapping case in which the Salt Lake City teenager was abducted by a homeless person.

In order to obtain a working understanding of both print and electronic media portrayals of the homeless and of homelessness, I read all of the stories. Two additional readers were used – one who read and coded all 2,300 stories and a second who read a sample of 25% of the stories and provided complete coding, including in-depth analysis for some stories. The sample was randomly selected from the 2,300 stories to provide a manageable volume of stories to analyze.

The two tables below illustrate how these data will later be used in the book for analysis and interpretation.

Table 1. Side-by-Side Comparison of Reader 1's and Reader 2's Results for Each Rating Factor, for Broadcast News Media.

Total	Reader 1				Broadcast Media	Reader 2				Total
	0	1	2	3		0	1	2	3	
25	6	7	8	4	ABC	3	7	9	5	24
22	5	5	3	9	CBS	6	8	2	8	24
50	13	20	3	14	CNN	12	21	4	14	51
25	7	2	3	13	Fox	6	3	4	11	24
21	4	5	5	7	NBC	3	9	2	8	22
143	35	39	22	47	288	30	48	21	46	145
49.7%	24.5%	27.3%	15.4%	32.9%		20.7%	33.1%	14.5%	31.7%	50.3%

Table 2. Side-by-Side Comparison of Reader 1's and Reader 2's Results for Each Rating Factor, for Print News Media.

Total	Reader 1				Print Media	Reader 2				Total
	0	1	2	3		0	1	2	3	
51	16	15	16	4	Alb Jrnl	8	19	21	3	51
182	66	52	56	8	NY Times	46	78	48	13	185
88	43	12	28	5	LA Times	19	36	26	7	88
321	125	79	100	17	645	73	133	95	23	324
49.8%	38.9%	24.6%	31.2%	5.3%		22.5%	41.0%	29.5%	7.1%	50.2%

Studying the output of the news media provides important data in terms of what information flows to the public, but it grants no insights into what people working in the news media know about homeless people or the status of homeless. Further, the output of the media provides no understanding of what opinions journalists may hold about homeless people and the condition of being homeless. Therefore, I identified a sample of journalists to interview.

The media personnel selected for interviews constituted a convenience sample. I contacted various members of the media with whom I have worked over the past several years. This form of sampling was used to take advantage of my prior professional relationships with journalists. Many journalists are reluctant to talk for publication about their work; some may fear reprisals by their employers or simply may be reluctant to be critical of the media in which they work. The prior experience with the selected journalists permitted me to elicit more straightforward response from journalists than likely would have been possible with a random sample of journalists who had little or no awareness of the researcher. I explained the research and asked them to participate in a brief interview to: a) talk about their personal coverage of the homeless, and b) address what appeared to them to be the issues of most concern to the homeless. This is the request sent to local media representatives to initiate contact:

"I am in the middle of a qualitative dissertation on how the media portray the homeless. The bulk of the research is revolving around a content analysis of articles written and pieces shown on the homeless by the *New York Times, Los Angeles Times, The Albuquerque Journal,* CBS, NBC, ABC, Fox News, CNN and MSNBC. One recurring theme that I found in my interviews with the homeless was a complaint that in their mind the media do not make enough attempts to understand the 'plight' of the homeless but rather choose to focus on the negative. Responding to that, one local anchor said he feels no more responsibility to the homeless than he does to any other group/cause/issue he covers. A theme of all the interviews I did with the homeless was that they wanted the media to hang out with them. It seems their perspective was/is the media should be more advocates than reporters. If you could address that and then share your random thoughts about how (you) cover the homeless and how the media and in general portray the homeless. Anything you say is helpful."

The audio of all interviews was digitally recorded and transcribed. Pertinent segments of the interviews are used as data in the study; however, the complete text of the interviews appears in Chapter 4 (broadcast and print journalists) and Appendices C and D (homeless).

Any study of homeless people and of the state of being homeless would be incomplete without involving the homeless. I selected a sample of homeless people. Nineteen of the homeless people who were interviewed were residents of the homeless shelter in Albuquerque, New Mexico called Joy Junction. I am executive director of Joy Junction, so in order to avoid any potential for intimidating the respondents or bias because of my position, interviews with residents of that shelter were conducted by a research assistant who used an interview guide that I developed. The individuals interviewed were members of Joy Junction's Life Skills Program, and they were not given a cash incentive for participating in the survey. They were at Joy Junction for some weeks, aiming to achieve an element of stability not observed in the individuals interviewed at other shelters in and around downtown Albuquerque.

I personally interviewed the additional 12 homeless people in the sample. They were homeless individuals who were receiving services at three downtown Albuquerque locations which serve the homeless. The service providers for the homeless were a) First United Methodist Church, a meal site for the homeless; b) Noon Day Ministries, an evangelical, faith-based ministry that provides lunch and a variety of other services for the homeless; and c) St. Martin's Hospitality Center, a non faith-based equivalent of Noon Day Ministries.

A board member of Albuquerque's Homeless Advocacy Coalition helped with the interviews conducted at the downtown locations. He scheduled and observed all the interviews, receiving compensation for his work. The interviewees at these locations were also given a small cash incentive for their participation.

The interviews with homeless people were designed to accomplish four goals: (1) to ask people who had been homeless until a few days or a few weeks before the interviews to describe how and why they had become homeless; (2) to obtain information about their assessment of their lives as homeless people; (3) to obtain their assessment of how the media covered homeless people; and (4) to obtain information on how they perceived that members of the dominant culture viewed people who were homeless.

Admittedly, the use of a random sample of homeless people would provide a considerable advantage over the use of a theoretical sample. However, pragmatically, there simply is no reasonable means for developing a sampling frame of the universe of homeless people in Albuquerque, or any other city, from which to draw a random sample. The typical devices used in identifying a universe of people – telephone directories, home addresses, list of employers, etc. – do not exist for homeless people.

4

Findings

This chapter primarily comprises highlights of interviews with 1) a national advocate for the homeless, 2) a theoretical sample of homeless individuals (the full interviews are presented in Appendix C), and 3) a number of broadcast and print media professionals from Albuquerque, New Mexico.

One goal of the research was to learn what homeless people themselves thought about their portrayal in the media. Interviewing a theoretical sample of the homeless was considered to be important, because it was necessary to determine the homeless population's perception of themselves as measured against the media's perception of the homeless population in general.

My research confirmed that the homeless individuals interviewed considered their plight to be inadequately represented and insensitively portrayed by the media. More specifically, most of those interviewed believed the media tended to over-report negative stories about them, e.g., criminal acts, and to under-report positive stories, e.g., individuals who were trying to improve their situations.

The data appear to support this view, at least with respect to the reporting by the broadcast media. When one looks at the aggregate content ratings of the broadcast and print media stories by two readers, a pattern emerges.

Table 3. Aggregate Content Ratings for All Reviewed News Stories for Each News Medium (Broadcast, Print)

Broadcast media (288 story transcripts)	Content ratings	Print media (645 stories)
22.6 %	0 (did not mention or deal with homelessness)	30.7 %
30.2 %	1 (mentioned the homeless/ homelessness peripherally)	32.9 %
14.9 %	2 (mentioned the homeless/ homelessness explicitly)	30.2 %
32.3 %	3 (reported criminal acts either by or against the homeless)	6.2 %

Interviews

Rev. Steve Burger, homeless advocate. An interview with Rev. Steve Burger, Executive Director of the Association of Gospel Rescue Missions (AGRM), is included due to the size and stature of AGRM (S. Burger, personal communication, February 10, 2004). An article on the organization's web site states, "Rescue missions comprise the Association of Gospel Rescue Missions, formerly the International Union of Gospel Missions (IUGM), which was founded in 1913. As measured by annual revenue, the 294 association member RESCUE missions would be the sixth largest nonprofit organization in the United States" (www.agrm.org/intro.html).

Rev. Burger said that most of his association's involvement with the national media occurs when calls come in concerning a story on which they are working. "Oftentimes they are looking for an illustration of a story they already have set, and believe in," Rev. Burger stated, "and are looking for someone to illustrate and/or approve their hypothesis. Rarely if ever do they ask us if what they are presenting is a true picture."

Rev. Burger gave an example that he said had occurred with NBC News. The network was putting together a story on formerly affluent people who had become homeless due to difficult economic circumstances. Rev. Burger said the reporter asked him if his organization could provide any examples of this phenomenon.

"I explained to them," said Burger, "that most people who fall into homelessness due to the economy are those who are already on the margins, and just barely making it in a good economy. But that was not the story they were telling."

Rev. Burger said that despite his locating a former military family (staying in an AGRM member mission) experiencing hard times basically due to job issues, the director of that shelter told Burger that was not what the NBC crew was looking for.

That family was too "blue collar," Burger said. "They wanted someone like a lawyer, doctor, professor, etc., who was now homeless. They had written the story, and just wanted us to confirm it with an illustration. I have often felt the same about the national print media. They have their story written and want a quote or personal story to fill it out. However, there have been parts of interviews where I felt the writer was trying to develop the story and was interested in learning from those in the field."

According to Rev. Burger, the most "outlandish" of these media requests came several years ago, when ABC called trying to locate a family living in a cornfield (reminiscent of the movie "Field of Dreams"). Burger said the network was putting together a story on rural homelessness.

"This certainly would be a great visual, having the whole family walking out of the cornfield," Burger said. "However, even the most needy homeless would not pick a cornfield with no shelter. It seems to me they were more interested in the visual than in the truth."

Rev. Burger said he has had other negative experiences with national media. He recalled dealing with a network camera crew when he was executive director of a local rescue mission. He said that the individuals had neither "empathy nor common courtesy."

According to Burger, the crew was filming in an overflow night sleeping area in the Seattle mission, where more than 100 men were getting ready to go to bed. "The news crew," he said, "just went up to people and pushed the microphone in their faces and were very aggressive. They did not take any instructions or advice from us, and it became a tense scene. My sense was they 'didn't give a rip'" (about the feelings or privacy of the people being filmed).

Rev. Burger stated that the local media do a better job of covering the homeless. "They have," he said, "a great deal of empathy for the homeless, and are sensitive to their situation."

Another factor Burger said he had experienced in his dealings with television and radio representatives, is that they are looking for someone who will oppose the viewpoint or program of the government. He said those willing to speak out against a government-sponsored program have an opportunity "to make it onto the news."

Stating that he has learned some valuable lessons in his dealings with the media, Burger continued: "I have tried to learn to speak to the media in short sound bites, for it doesn't seem they are really interested in 'who are the homeless' if it takes more than 15 seconds to explain it. They want quick, simple answers to difficult, complex problems. They ask a loaded question like, 'Why is this administration giving such a low count on the number of homeless, while others are giving numbers three and four times higher?' If I try to talk about 'who' each group is counting as the homeless, their eyes glaze over."

Summary of Interviews with the Homeless, by Themes

Because of the number of responses from the homeless, they are not included in this part of the book, but are summarized instead.

Thematic overview. The interviews are divided into predominant themes. Those themes are: a) media personnel need to spend more time with the homeless, b) the media need to spend more time covering the work done by homeless shelters, c) the media spend too much time covering the problematic homeless and not the ones who want to improve, d) the media's coverage of the homeless is negative and needs to improve, e) it is the media's responsibility to help the homeless find employment, f) the media should provide year-round coverage of the homeless – not only during the Thanksgiving and Christmas seasons, g) the media should get their stories about the homeless directly from the homeless, not from another source, h) it is important for reporters not to begin with a negative attitude, i) the media's coverage of the homeless is not negative, but a "cry for help," j) there needs to be better communication between the media and the homeless.

By far the most frequent theme, as articulated by 17 out of the 31 homeless respondents, was that the media representatives need to spend more time with the homeless in order to adequately portray their plight.

As one homeless respondent (31) said, "I think all cops and media and counselors need to take a 30-day course in Homeless 101. Just live out there with just the clothes on their back and find out how hard it is, with sore feet and knees and backs and arms, to get from point A to point B. If they have to, learn how to panhandle or pick stuff up off the ground to make ends meet. (They should) live there themselves and see for themselves what it really takes to find a warm spot where you're not gonna be harassed by the police department."

Three respondents said the media need to spend more time covering the work done by homeless shelters.

One of them (4) stated: "They ought to be coming out and researching it," he said. "Go shelter by shelter and see what people have to offer to the homeless people, and how they can help them. They ought to at least look into (what) the people are doing ... for the homeless and find out why they're doing it and what they can offer."

Three respondents said the media focus on covering the problematic homeless and not the ones who want to improve their situations.

One respondent (11) suggested. "I wish they (the media) would come out here and do some of the little pieces they do for the people off the streets on some of us, and try and help us, the people that really want and need the help – the people that just can't quite get ahead in life because it's too hard, but they want to. I wish they would come out here and show a homeless person that's struggling to do good, to do things right, instead of a homeless person that's gonna go drink their life away, or smoke their life away."

Three respondents said the media's coverage of the homeless is negative and, in their opinion, needs to improve.

One of them (30) put it like this: "I don't think the media understands that the majority of the homeless people don't want to be homeless; it's just the situation that they're in. Sometimes they stay homeless, and sometimes they get off the street. It just depends on the individual. The ones that are trying is the ones that the media makes it hard for them."

Asked how the media "make it hard" for the homeless, he replied, "Because they think (about) the ones that aren't trying, (and that's) negative, (instead of) the ones that are, and then they think that everybody's not trying to get off the street."

Two thought it was the media's responsibility to help them find employment. One respondent (3) put it like this: "Help us out with the job if there's one available ... Give us work. Give us a chance. Don't judge us by how we look. Just because we dress in old ratty jeans and a T-shirt and coats don't mean we're bad people."

One respondent (12) said that the media should provide year-round coverage of the homeless – not just during the Thanksgiving and Christmas seasons. He put it like this: "We're not just homeless during November and December; we're homeless through the year. They need to give us the same coverage they give us during November and December ... because you know, Joy

Junction lives on donations and without that, we don't eat. We aren't clothed, we don't have roofs over our head, the light and utilities don't get paid, so the media needs to take the same approach to the homeless year round that they take two months of the year. They should be year round instead of just November and December."

One respondent (17) suggested the media should get their stories about the homeless directly from the homeless – not someone else. He said: "Second hand information is the worst kind ... of information. It's families, doctors, lawyers, Indian chiefs, all become homeless. Go up to that individual and ... maybe more people will be willing to help out."

Another respondent (22) said it is important for reporters covering the homeless not to begin with a negative attitude. He said, "Step (up) to the situation with an open mind, because not every homeless person is in the same situation as the next homeless person. When you step to a homeless person and you speak negative toward them, you're going to get a negative response. You step up to a homeless person and you don't have to have a sympathetic ear, or have a sympathetic heart. Have a sympathetic well being, so to speak, and try to see eye-to-eye with that person, because you never know if you're in that situation what you're looking at."

One person said he considered the media's coverage of the homeless as not being negative, but more of "a cry for help." That respondent (5) put it like this, "There are definitely (bad and good) ... in every group ... If they do show a lot of homeless people, some of them are not trying to help themselves. They're in the system, so people need to be educated to know that there are people that want to get back into society, so to speak. And I think they should show that type of person more."

Interviews with National Media Professionals

The purpose here is to determine whether the homeless population's concern – as expressed by their opinions in the interviews – is correct, that the media's depiction of them could lead the general population to view the media portrayals of the plight of the homeless as accurate, no matter how incorrect and incomplete they actually may be.

International journalist. An interview with Dan Wooding (D. Wooding, personal communication, February 13, 2004), an international journalist whose ASSIST News Service has provided coverage of worldwide humanitarian issues for many years, yielded the following opinion:

"I don't think the problem is *how* the media covers the homeless, but why they don't cover this important topic. Maybe the answer lies in the fact that much of the idea is celebrity-driven, and so they would prefer not to cover this troubling topic. Ratings for much of the media are important and so they don't see the need to report on those whom they see as being at the bottom of the heap. Homelessness is a modern-day tragedy, but the greater tragedy is the callousness of our American media in walking by on the other side, when they could be exploring the needs of the homeless and helping to provide some solutions."

Christian editor / journalist. Marvin Olasky, professor, journalist and editor of the evangelical Christian "World" Magazine, agreed to be interviewed for this study (M. Olasky, personal communication, March 2, 2004). Olasky is recognized for his book, *The Tragedy of American Compassion*, which deals with the changing approach over the last 100 years to dealing with poverty.

Olasky wrote that reporters typically talk about "the homeless" without understanding how diverse the people in that category are, so in that sense, some time spent cultivating a better understanding of the homeless milieu would help. "It would be important, though," he said, "to ask hard questions and not merely accept rationales."

According to Olasky, reporters routinely see all homeless individuals as victims and rarely seek another perspective. "Some (particularly women and children abandoned by husbands and fathers) are in that situation for reasons beyond their control, but many are perpetrators: they've made themselves homeless because of their actions. Both victims and perps (and some are both) need help, but different kinds of help, and that rarely comes through in media reports."

Interviews with Local Media Professionals

Albuquerque Broadcast Reporter Number 1 (personal communication, February 7, 2004). A local network affiliate television reporter and anchor was asked how she thought the media cover the homeless, both locally and nationally. "I don't think we do cover it, and I think there's a couple of reasons for that," she said. "I think we do it infrequently when it's something big, like a homeless person is accused of stabbing the person who was using the telephone," she said. "The homeless guy came up and asked him for a quarter; he said, 'no, I'm not giving you a quarter,' and [the homeless guy] stabbed him. So I think we cover it in that way just because we have to. If it weren't a homeless person, if it was anybody, I think we would have done the story. I don't think it matters they were homeless. It might make it a little more interesting because they maybe showed the angle of how they needed the money a little bit more, but in general, I don't think we cover the homeless much at all."

However, she added that, in her opinion, there is good reason for that lack of coverage. "It's the way the TV business is," she said. "It's not a sexy story, the video is horribly boring, they see people sitting around on the side of the street and nothing moving. We in TV have to look for good video opportunities, and if it's not a 'zowie-wowie' interesting topic that's something new, or interesting video, we don't like to cover it."

This reporter talked about her wish to do stories about the homeless when she arrived at the station about three-and-a-half years ago. "I thought, 'Let's go and spend the night with these homeless people, let's see where they get their food from,' and I thought it would be a great story. And I still do, though not as much, but I still want to do that story, and (our news director said), 'nobody cares.'"

Explaining her motivation, she continued, "I wanted to do these guys that sleep under the bridges, near Lead and Coal out near 25. You just see those rolled-up beds there, those are the people I want to see, to ask 'em why they don't go get help from all the facilities that are around, if they're drinking too much and that's why they can't get into shelters."

Commenting on the rationale that apparently underlies much of television news, this anchor explained, "I still want to do that story, but because it's not 'sexy,' and I say that very loosely. (However), our news director didn't want to cover it at the time and I don't think our new news director wants to, either. She said, 'After all, what's new?'"

Continuing, she said, "It's the same story we've been doing 10 years ago when we followed the homeless people, so I think that's one reason we don't cover it. How does it affect people is another reason. We always look for stories that affect people, and sometimes they don't. Sometimes they're crime stories that don't affect anybody and they're just quirky or interesting. Homelessness doesn't affect many people, and I say that with a grain of salt, because I know homelessness is a big problem that I think we all need to work on."

She went on, "Viewers see the issue of homelessness 'selfishly.' They think, 'That homeless person doesn't affect me, doesn't come in contact with me,' and they won't care as viewers, and that's why we don't cover the homeless people."

This reporter said that she absolutely does not feel "obligated" to cover the homeless. "I know some people have gotten some bad breaks and I know they're on the streets because of a number of reasons, sometimes, a lot of times for mental reasons, and I don't feel one bit sorry for those people. I refuse to give them money on the street corners. I will donate to a shelter like Joy Junction, but I refuse to help these people on the street because my perception is that they're going to be buying booze or drugs (and) not … doing anything good with it."

She continued, "The hostility exhibited by some of the homeless toward the media further serves to exacerbate the difficulty of coverage. When there's a story about panhandling (and) … we go either to try to get video of people just trying to get a few extra dollars on the streets, or shooting video of homeless people, they are very hostile. 'Get that camera away from me, I want nothing to do with you.' We say, 'Well, talk to us about your situation and why it works for you' and they don't even want to talk to you. As soon as they see you, they get this instant attitude, 'Get the hell away from me, you guys are all bad.'"

However, she did have a pleasant experience when doing one story about panhandling. After an Albuquerque panhandling ordinance passed, the reporter described finding "the nicest gentleman." According to her, "He held up a card with a picture of a kitty cat that says, 'We all need help, thank you, God bless you.' He talked to us on camera … and said, 'I have medical bills, I just come out here when I need help with my medical bills.' Now that could have been BS; I don't know. But I felt a little more sympathetic because he explained his story. We used him on TV and he was fabulous," she said.

This man told the reporter that he doesn't approach anyone. "If they want to give me money, that's their prerogative," he said. "I don't bother anybody and I don't push anybody. I don't feel they're obligated to give me money. (But) if they want to, I'm here to take it."

After that, the reporter said, "I kind of got a different look at it from his point of view and I was thinking, 'You know what, I feel sorry for this guy,' and I've given him dog bones (for his dog) every time I see him."

She continued, "In general, you're going to see a lot more negative news on the TV than positive news. That's what gets people interested. If you gave them 10 minutes of feature stories, they don't care. People say they don't care about crime, but statistics have shown that whenever there's a crime story on, they're tuned in and watching. There's been a ton of research done on this. So I think negative news in general, and I don't think it matters whether it's homeless, the police department, the mayor's office, your neighbor down the street, in general, that's the way (it is). Negativity just exists in TV."

Regarding the contention by a number of homeless people interviewed for this research that the media need to see how they live, she responded, "There's no way in a million years I'm going to spend three days sitting around the campfire getting to know these people. And I hate to say it, but I don't know if our average viewer cares. I think people truly would tune out if they saw the life of a homeless person. They'd probably say, 'You know what, I don't care.' I think the attitude is, 'Get a job, get some help, go to Joy Junction, whatever you need to do to get your services to get yourself back on the street.' So I don't feel obligated to these people. Most of the time I don't care about their story, unless there's something positive coming out of a facility that's trying to help somebody … but I'm looking for something positive in that yucky negative situation. In general, I don't think people care … about the homeless."

She suggested that the best way to get coverage is through an established homeless agency. "Because if they came here and approached us at the station and said, 'Hey, I'm ready to talk to you, I would like to do a story about the homeless,' we'd tell them to 'Get the hell out of here, you're crazy' … It's so rare that we would approach them on the streets anyway, unless we were doing a panhandling story or something that's coming up in the news," she said.

"However," she added, "a phone call to a reporter at the station may set the ball rolling. If a homeless person was to call and say something to the effect of, 'Hey, you know what, I've got a good story. I'm a homeless person and I'd like to tell you my side of it.'"

However, the reporter said, the story idea needs to be something other than allegedly being roughed up by a cop. "You don't know how many times a day we hear, 'a cop beat me up; they're not listening to me. I'm a homeless guy,'" she said. "I tune out immediately to that because I've heard it a bazillion times. The accusations fly left and right. So I think if they called up (and said) … 'there's a facility here that's trying to help me out and it didn't; could you do a story on that,' or, 'there's a really good facility and it helped me out, could you do a story on that,' I might be more willing to look into that phone call."

This reporter said she would probably tell the person to give her their name and how she could get in touch with them. "We're not out here trying to do negative stories on homeless purposely," she said. "It's what sells." She emphasized that a homeless person calling in a legitimate news tip would not get turned down just because they happened to be homeless. "It does not matter whether they're homeless or have jobs or are millionaires," she said. "If something happens on the streets or there's something that we deem newsworthy, we don't care who you are, we're doing the story."

Summing up, the anchor said that the problem with television news covering homelessness is that nothing really changes. "The video is incredibly boring … and that's why I think you don't get a lot of coverage in TV news," she said. "Newspaper – I think you can dive in a little deeper to some issues; there's a little more time, a little more space in the newspaper. Here, we've got a minute to do a big long story we're doing, and we're not gonna commit that to the homeless unless there's something good going on. So it's unfortunate that we don't cover it a lot; I just think it would bore people to death."

She added that, while her newsroom is admittedly willing to listen to allegations, being willing to go on camera is key to a story getting on the air. "A lot of people don't want to go on camera to tell their story. They just want to tell you about their accusations and complaints and problems," she said. "I think in general the public's got a negative view of the homeless because they're always being asked for money … I think they see the negative side of homelessness, and that's why they also don't care about seeing these stories."

The anchor interviewed here was one of several journalists who used the term "sitting around the campfire." The use of this concept as a metaphor for sitting with a group of homeless people seems rather value-laden. Middle-class and upper-middle-class Americans are most likely to think of a campfire as a component of a camping trip or some other discretionary activity. Thus, when they use that concept to label the activities of homeless people, people who have homes and jobs are reflecting a somewhat elitist view of the homeless. For homeless people, building a fire usually is necessary to prepare food. Secondarily, the fire might also become a focus of a few homeless people conversing with each other during or after a meal, but the fire is not an optional activity. The journalists talked to did not understand that the use of a campfire among the homeless is not analogous to a group of well-off people going camping or otherwise engaging in some recreational activity.

Albuquerque Broadcast Reporter Number 2 (personal communication, February 8, 2004). Another reporter from the same network news affiliate was asked whether she believed that the media have a responsibility to get to know the homeless. She said that she thinks they do, "because oftentimes we do rely on press releases and people informing us of story ideas, and oftentimes homeless people do not know how to approach the media."

This reporter said that dealing with the issues of homelessness (as opposed to homeless people) is difficult. "It's kind of like, where do you go, where do you start, because there's no real breaking news." She continued, "When there is breaking news about a homeless person, it usually revolves around someone who has been killed."

"It's harder to find that deeper issue," she said. "And we're looking for that kind of news peg, probably something that's an injustice, somebody who's been wronged, and many times, it's not somebody who's homeless who knows how to approach the media to tell us about that. So usually it's the other party, and we end up doing stories that look more negative about homeless people." Continuing, "Regardless of who they are, the media have a responsibility to every person. Whether they're homeless or a business executive, it's our job as media representatives to find where there are stories that need to be told. And it's just harder to find them when there are issues, when they have to deal with something surrounding homelessness. Should we be going and sitting by them, sitting around the campfire and maybe talking to someone who's homeless? Perhaps – that's an option."

However, this reporter described some of the constraints with which she is faced as a broadcast journalist. She related how she spends her day at work. "It consists of breaking news. I'm constantly listening to (police radio) scanners, getting thrown on the latest story or press conference. Do I have time to sit down and think about issues and think about, brainstorm ideas? No, that's not my role. There's other people at my station who can do that role. My job as a reporter is to respond to the breaking news and to be thrown onto a story that's tossed my way."

Although she is sometimes called upon to offer ideas and could offer an opinion surrounding homelessness, this reporter said, "If it's not breaking, guaranteed I won't be doing it." But that philosophy can change around the quarterly ratings periods, called "sweeps" by the stations. "Then we have to go more in-depth, sure, they'll be more willing to say, 'Okay, let's do an investigative piece,' or 'Do something surrounding an issue.' But again, it has to have that news peg surrounding 'Why are we doing this now and what's the issue?' and 'Are we uncovering some kind of an injustice here? Why exactly are we doing this story?' And if I don't have an answer, then we won't do it."

According to her, an inability to effectively approach the media can also result in lack of coverage. "There are so many different kinds of groups, not just homeless people, who do not know how to approach the media and to phrase story ideas to us. So we are going off of our individual perceptions of what is news and what is out there and what needs to be told." She went on, "We're all very different people, but if we don't come from a background where we've covered or dealt with somebody who's homeless, of course we're going to lack in that area telling stories that deal with that (issue). But there are so many other areas that we lack in. We're just people out there seeing stories as we go, and if the right person doesn't talk to us, then the stories don't get told."

This reporter agreed – but with a qualification – to the charge made by the homeless that they are "picked on" by the media. She said, "That's right. We pick on everybody. At least that's the way I see it. Because the way news is conducted now, on local television, even on national television, we have to have something that's newsworthy as far as finding that latest news peg, finding something that's breaking right now, and most of the time, it's bad news. And so most of the time, our stories are bad news."

"Reporters are discouraged from covering 'happy news,'" she asserted, "because most of the time, so they are told, people tune in for 'hard news.' And what does that 'hard news' consist of?" she asked rhetorically. "It means," she said, "I'm covering injustices and it's always going to slam somebody. So it's going to be (about) a teacher, or a professional. We don't target homeless people; we don't say, 'Let's go and make these people look bad.'"

She added that, when someone comes to her with an accusation, she needs reliable facts from reliable sources. "If someone comes to me and says, 'The police did this, this and this to me,' I will say, 'Do you have proof?' 'No.' 'Do you any evidence?' 'No.' 'Do you have anything that can help me here – anything – any witnesses?' 'No.' So where do I go? I have a responsibility to the police as well to make sure I tell their side fairly. And I want to tell this other (homeless) person's story fairly, and I can't do that if I don't have a reliable source," she said.

Asked whether the media should be advocates for the homeless, this reporter replied, "There's a fine line between being responsible for telling stories and being advocates for telling stories," she said. "My job is to be responsible in telling the stories. If I have a story idea, I need to be sure I tell it accurately and fairly on all sides and make sure my facts are straight. Am I an advocate for either party? Never … That's rule number one in journalism. I'm nobody's advocate. Am I supposed to tell stories in regards to homeless people? Sure. But I have to tell them fairly and reliably. (If I can't), then I won't tell them. I would rather err on the side of not telling them than telling stories I know would be biased from the beginning."

Addressing the frequent homeless refrain of alleged police abuse, she said that if somebody homeless comes to her and complains about "police brutality," this is how she thinks."If I start to hear a trend, I'd better be on that story, because I do have a responsibility to uncover that. If police are doing something that's wrong, maybe we should take our hidden cameras and go down there and try to find that evidence for them. But if I have one person coming to me with one story, and they have not a lot of information to back it up, knowing the breaking news business of television, I'm just going to let it go."

She contended that many homeless people have the wrong idea of how they are viewed by the media. "I don't view them as stupid or unreliable at all times. I think they're very valid people, but they just don't know how to come to us to present their information," she said. "If somebody were to come up to me off the street, my first impression would probably be, 'Why are they on the street?' And (I'd think), ... 'why aren't they doing something about it?' Do I want to help them? Of course, but I'm not going to be their advocate. That's not my job. I wish they wouldn't assume that we're out to get them. I am more than willing to help them out if I know where to go with what they're saying."

How should the homeless approach this reporter to engender her sympathy? "With reliable information substantiated by more than one source," she said, continuing, "Perhaps go to a homeless advocacy group that can support their claims and then approach the media as a group instead of as an individual. Come to us with story ideas. We talk in story ideas. That's our language, and they need to understand that the media deals with deadlines, and needs to have story angles and that kind of thing."

Concluding, she said, "I think sometimes homeless advocacy groups can help in that regards, because they've dealt with the media and they're kind of the bridge way. I've had to do stories with homeless people. Do I shy away from them? No way. I would be more than happy to do a story on anything and everything 'cause that's my job. I'm inquisitive and curious about every single topic that's out there. But if there's no story there, then my job's done. There's nowhere to go."

Albuquerque Broadcast Reporter Number 3 (personal communication, February 10, 2004). Another anchor of a local network news affiliate described both the local and national homeless situations as "far more complex than any of us really understand." He said that, in his opinion, "Just to lump all the homeless under the banner of one word is unfair, because there are so many different populations of homeless people."

He labeled past coverage of the homeless as "incredibly superficial and said, "it remains that in a lot of ways, because I don't know if it's as issue oriented and solution oriented as it should be. If homeless people get coverage in this city, now, it continues to be homeless feeds, and most recently it's been panhandling. Then the third element is the homeless who are possibly freezing to death in the winter and need a place to stay."

In responding to the frequently voiced complaint from the homeless that they are victims of a lot of negative coverage, he stated, "That's in many respects the way news is; what happens everyday that works out okay is not what news is. It's some of the negative things that happen that tend to get our attention. And the homeless probably get more negative attention than many because they may be more desperate, they may be on drugs or alcohol, and we tend to zero in on some of the actions that they're responsible for that aren't so good."

This anchor said he felt no need to go sit around the campfire with the homeless so he could better understand them, as had been suggested by some homeless people. "What's the point of that?" he asked. "Why do I want to go under a bridge and sit around a campfire for eight to ten hours getting to know the homeless? I don't do that with anyone else, really."

The anchor said, "Life is inherently painful, and it's a struggle for everyone, whether it's a homeless person or some man or woman who's marching off to their job and working 45 to 50 hours a week. I don't necessarily have a great amount of sympathy for – and I say this personally and as a journalist – for someone who may choose to be homeless." He continued, "As we get more sophisticated covering these stories, there's a huge difference between someone who may choose that as a lifestyle and someone who is homeless because of some circumstances. Someone who is homeless for a while, not for the rest of their life, and … if you're down and out, but you're genuinely making a significant effort to be employed so you can take care of yourself and your children, I applaud you. I really do. And I think society does in general."

"However," this anchor said, "if, for whatever reason, you're standing at a street corner when you could be working and you've got a sign and you're trying to scam me, I don't want to sit around a campfire with you and exchange stories and feel sorry for you. That's just the way it is. And one thing we all need to remember is that journalists are people, and in general they're pretty smart people, and they're skeptical and they don't want to be scammed – like the rest of the population … We've got the memory of an elephant in some ways."

What would he say to a homeless person who says that he or she doesn't choose to be homeless and that their plight is the result of a difficult economy? He responded, "George Bush's economic policies affect me, too, and they affect my neighbor, and they affect the person in the South Valley. There is a segment of the population that is possibly victimized, and maybe they do lose their jobs. But you know what? A lot of those folks are pounding on the door every day trying to get jobs. Maybe if they don't get a job after a year or two or three, they're disillusioned and might become homeless, and that is a different deal. I feel for those people. But we're all living in a society where we're all affected by certain influences, whether they be political or otherwise, and you just have to do your best to survive in this cruel world."

The anchor said, "The safety net for homeless people is a heck of a lot more expansive than you might think." He continued, "There are a lot of places to go, and I know there are homeless people who get hooked into that, because it's possible to survive with all the help that's out there and to do okay. But I want to make the clear distinction that there is a difference between the homeless population that has chosen that as a way of life and that huge chunk of the homeless society that's trying their damndest to be productive. And those people need help, because you know what? Even though I've got a great job and I make a lot of money, I'm potentially one firing away, one rating point away, from not having a job myself and maybe needing some help."

He suggested that the media's coverage of the homeless could perhaps be improved by being less simplistic. "I don't know if we have taken a comprehensive look at homelessness and what resources are out there to help the people who really need the help," he said. "We probably need to do that. I will also tell you that, though, in some ways I think the viewing audience, and it may be in part the way we've covered stories in the past, is possibly a little numb and maybe turned off to homeless stories because of the way they've been covered in the past."

This anchor addressed a situation probably not considered by the homeless and other groups when they see their issue not receiving the coverage they believe it merits – the lack of staff in the newsroom. He said that is "a practical concern every minute of our existence." He added, "There are so many stories out there to cover, and through research and ratings, we've discovered that the viewers want a certain story. They want late-breaking live stories, which, whether you agree with it or not, is our bread and butter. So there may be some stories on the fringe, and some homeless stories may fit into that category, that probably deserve some attention. But just because of the resources we have or don't have, we may not be able to get someone out there to cover it. In other words, sometimes the homeless stories may be a little lower on the ladder of importance.

"For the homeless to be upset with me that I don't sit around the campfire and get to know them is, in my mind, greedy in some ways, or selfish ... Accountants and plumbers and firefighters and police officers could be asking the same thing. In many ways, they deserve just as much time as the homeless do. Just because of our business, we don't spend a whole lot of time with any particular group."

The anchor concluded by saying, "If I'm reincarnated and I get a another shot at this, maybe I as a journalist and a person can spend more time getting to know the homeless, but first time around, I'm struggling to know myself, and know my wife and my kids, and know a little bit about every single story we cover. And that's all I can really do. And I don't know that the homeless deserve any more time than those in homes and those working really hard. I will do what I can to understand them. But it's a two-way street."

Reminiscing, he added, "I remember this time when we did a public service announcement promoting some sort of holiday meal for the homeless, and we went to St. Martin's (a local day shelter for the homeless). They sat us down at a table with some homeless people and we were delivering our lines, and up from this table jumps one of the homeless men, basically saying, 'Who the hell do you think you are? You're so uppity, we need help. We don't need your sympathy,' and it was very shocking to me. I was trying to do something to help them."

Albuquerque Broadcast Reporter (Photo Journalist) Number 4 (personal communication, February 14, 2004). A photojournalist from a network news affiliate was asked what he thought of the media coverage of the homeless. He responded, "I think the media cover the homeless the way we cover a lot of things ... we focus on the negative in everything. I think the news is kinda negative and people have asked for that. When you do ratings surveys, when they asked the public, when you have too many features and you go too soft, people don't watch your show."

The photojournalist said what that shows is that as much as people complain about the proliferation of crime on television, they nonetheless tune into it. "There's a fascination with bad things," he said. "It's unfortunate, but when you hear about the homeless in the media, oftentimes you're hearing about a small percentage of the homeless, but like with a lot of things, that's (the case). I think the media could do a whole lot better."

Asked whether the media are in any way obligated to cover the homeless, the photojournalist said perhaps publicly funded media like PBS are, but the networks are another matter. "As far as the networks, it's privately owned, it's ratings driven, it's advertising driven, and unfortunately, a lot of people would say, we're not advertising to the homeless," he said. "I've actually heard management say things like that. We've got a paying viewing public and we need to advertise to them, and some management are very cold to anyone that's not being advertised to."

Regarding whether there is still a way for the media to improve their coverage of the homeless, given those parameters, he suggested, "Maybe if we had a Democrat in office, we'd be responding more to it, because ... in my view then we have a more sympathetic government, but I don't know, because it's hard to get past the private ownership thing. It's hard to get past these people that are only thinking of ratings and small gains in advertising prices based on that. So I don't know."

He said he thought it would help media coverage of the homeless for reporters to "hang out" with them for a while, because he had actually done so in the past. "I did a fascinating interview where I hung out under the

Lead overpass in a little camp there and got to talk to some people, and people came out of their little tents. I think it helps, but you've got to find the right media people to go in and do that. A lot of people aren't willing to do that," he said. "There are a lot of people out there who are intimidated by the homeless. Some people, their only contact with the homeless is the ones they run into on the street who are yelling at them, and again, that's a drag, because that's a very small percentage. Those people are seeing the worst, so that's their view of things. But those are the ones who come up and bother me on my live shots. The worst of them. Just these few people, they're the same people. They're kind of messing it up for a lot of other people, and we shouldn't be focusing on them, it's too bad that we do. Because it's a very important (issue)."

"However," he added, returning to the realities and constraints of his job, "I don't know what the media could do. You've got to get past the pig-headed management that's only looking in the short-run. We're supposed to be local and this is what's happening locally. If I was news director, we'd be doing things different. But maybe then my ratings would be bad."

Because ratings result in advertising dollars, they play a key role in decision making. As this photojournalist said, "you can't ignore the advertising dollars because the overhead is so much. It's expensive to put TV on, especially in a situation like ours (at a network affiliate). We're completely advertising driven, because we're not a cable channel … The advertising is everything and it decides everything. If our advertising rates go down, I could lose my job … It's a very vicious cycle. I don't know, as far as accountability, certainly public TV should be all over this."

Albuquerque Broadcast Reporter Number 5 (personal communication, February 16, 2004). Another network affiliate reporter said he had heard some news directors say they weren't terribly interested in covering the homeless because a lot of them feel many of the homeless choose to be out there on their own. "I've heard that many times," he said. "But I think there are other people who don't choose to be that way. They're down on their luck and truly trying to do something. I think you have to cover the homeless like any societal problem."

"Homelessness is a community problem," this reporter said, "and we're part of the community, so we should probably be doing (something). I won't call it equal time, but we're part of the community, and I think we need to address their concerns and some of the problems they have, but on the other hand, I think there are some people who don't want to cover that as much because they think they're not as big a deal as other issues going on."

"Some stories are going to make news regardless of who is responsible," the reporter continued. "We'll hear of a homeless panhandler who attacks somebody; that's probably gonna make press even if it wasn't a homeless person, or somebody asking for money who maybe has a home. But I think that for the most part, we try to be well-rounded," he asserted.

To help the homeless successfully communicate with the media, this reporter suggested that maybe an "advocate" could be helpful. "A lot of times we don't know about some of the things that happen, and people sometimes assume we're going to know or we should know, when we really don't know," he said. "So sometimes it's somebody actually bringing it to our attention. So if there's a homeless advocate group or person that we can contact (and ask), 'hey, is there anything going on today with your group?,' I think that would be a help. That way we'd know what's going on."

He said he was unaware of complaints by some homeless individuals that not enough was being done to publicize their plight. "If the public demanded that we do more, if we got surveys back and they said they wanted to hear more about the homeless, or those kind of issues, I'm sure we'd consider doing more than we do now," he said. "I guess somebody calling in and saying, 'Hey I heard about this homeless story,' or 'Why don't you do more homeless stories?'"

Acknowledging that he had been thinking that people's perception of who the homeless are – people with blankets walking down the street and a long line of people gathering at a local church for an upcoming free lunch – isn't necessarily correct, he had this to say.

"I think there's another side," he said. "I've been to a homeless shelter and seen families with kids over there. I think probably one thing (that would shock) a lot of people … is the kid factor in the homeless. All these families. But again, we don't see that all the time, so maybe people don't know it's as much of a problem as it is."

Albuquerque Print Reporter Number 1 (personal communication, February 17, 2004). A veteran print reporter for *The Albuquerque Journal* had strong feelings about the suggestion that for reporters to understand the homeless, they had to live among them.

"It's not necessarily true," he said. "That's like saying you can't understand what it's like to be a drug addict unless you were one. You can't understand what it's like to be a soldier unless you were in Vietnam. If you were a supply clerk someplace else, you somehow had an incomplete experience, right? I think that's a misconception ... I don't believe that I need to experience everything first hand in order to know that they're good, bad or indifferent. I can read about them; I can hear other people's opinions. I mean, we live in the Information Age. I can do a Google search on any topic you can think of and come up with a veritable encyclopedia of information, and based upon that information, I can formulate some sort of opinion. I don't have to be homeless to know how difficult it must be for many of these people. I can imagine that."

Asked whether, as a print reporter, he felt he had an easier job covering the homeless than a broadcast journalist, he said he did and explained why. He explained that, while many people who are homeless for reasons beyond their control want to talk about their situations, they nonetheless don't want to be a "talking head" on the late news. "I think the people who want the media attention from the television stations are the ones who are slightly off, who don't have as much invested in changing their situation so that they're no longer homeless," he said. They're "the ones who are perfectly content to keep things as they are, because it's easier to complain about it than it is to do something about it."

Regarding whether the media should be advocates for the homeless, he said, "We're not advocates ... And we don't become an advocacy organization, because if we become an advocacy organization, then we can't be taken seriously as a credible media outlet. So the idea of being an advocate is something I think the homeless would like us to do, as much as they would like us, in their mind, to stop looking at their drug addictions and alcoholism. But that's a myth, too. We don't look at that either. I mean, that's part of who they are, and occasionally when we write stories about people and it results in something positive, some benefit coming to them, that's good, but it's not because we're advocating for them. It's because we're trying to explain this multi-faceted problem of 'the homeless.'"

"As such," he continued, "the homeless person or people featured in the story may benefit from what is being said." But that wasn't the reason for writing the story.

"Now there is something called 'service' journalism, which we do practice, and you find that in the Sunday 'Reach Out' page every Sunday," he said. "And that's where you highlight people who are doing stuff in the community, people who have taken up causes and they're trying to be part of the solution and not part of the problem. That section," this reporter said, "is clearly identified as 'service journalism.' It's where you try to identify problems in the community and highlight not only those problems, but also the people (and) … what they're doing. It's little personality profiles of these people. Who they are, what are their organizations about, how do they go about helping other people, and even that's not like the Journal advocating."

According to this reporter, the media's mission is one of "public information. We want the public to know that this is happening in their own backyard. This is happening in their own community, and especially with (a series like) 'Help for the Holidays' that we do every year, we're inviting the readers to say to themselves, 'Okay, now that I know what the problem is, what can I do to be part of the solution, as opposed to just feeding into the problem?'"

He said, "I think we're doing as good a job (of reporting on the homeless) and giving it as much attention as we can. Really, though, as serious as the problem of homelessness in America is, there are other things to report on. I mean, how much time can we spend?" He added, "Now, one legitimate complaint is why is there an increased amount of attention on the homeless problem only during the holidays? And I think that's true to some extent. The *Albuquerque Journal* reports on the problem throughout the year, and I can't speak for the other media. But we do report on the problem throughout the year, and there is an increased emphasis throughout the holidays. Why do we do that? Because we know that when most people respond … And I think you know that, too … that's when the bulk of your donations happen, isn't it? So we're aware of that and we're trying to help you guys," this reporter asserted. "We're not trying to advocate for you; it's not our job to advocate, but if you're going to write a story, you want to write a story when it's going to have the most impact. The reason we do it then, I think, is because we know that's when people respond most positively to it."

He said that while his paper is careful not "to beat people over the head too much during the year" with stories about homelessness, at the same time editors know that the problem is year-round. "But the increased focus, the concentrated focus, is during the holidays because a) that's when most people respond to it, and b) because we don't want to keep reinventing the wheel over and over again because people just tune you out," he said.

In the late 1980's, this print reporter spent a few days and nights on the streets trying to get a handle on just who the homeless were. He explained what he found then and some of what he experienced. "I stayed in some of the shelters, and I spent a lot of time out in the streets," he said. "The Journal, by the way, did make some generous donations to those shelters and organizations where I appeared, so it wasn't like I was eating their food and sleeping in their beds, and just sort of exploiting them ... But the idea for the story was to get a handle on who the homeless were. It wasn't to confirm there was a homeless problem, we knew that there was."

He continued, "I found there was a professional class of homeless people, who actually keep a log of how many miles they travel a year. It's like a game to them, and they know exactly what shelters are in which cities, what services they provide, how long they can stay there and when the seasons change in these different areas ... I would call this people professional homeless; that's what they do."

He next talked about what insights he gained into the issue of homelessness. "I found out there's kind of a pecking order among the homeless. Even among the homeless, there are certain groups of homeless people who they try to stay away from. One of those was the sniffers, the huffers," he said.

He elaborated. "I don't speak Spanish, but there was a homeless guy and he and I were watching this take place underneath a bridge. These guys got into an argument over something. There were some verbal exchanges insulting somebody else's mother and their heritage. Apparently ... it just got out of hand, and there was some construction debris lying around and they started picking up pieces of cinder blocks and discarded two by four's and just started whaling on each other. These people and people like them, these people who sniffed paint and I guess other substances, even the homeless people who had other issues, stayed away from them. So I hadn't realized that there was a pecking order among the homeless, but apparently there is, or was."

As a feature writer he said he would certainly be willing to spend more time on the streets, but one of the questions his editors would want to know would be what the "payoff" would be. "Is there going to be some new information, some new insight that we don't already have about the homeless? And I'm not sure that I could guarantee them that sort of outcome. I'm not sure that they'd want their resources spent in that way," he said.

This writer denied the charge that the media ignore the "daily plight" of the homeless. He said, "I think there has to be a limit to how much you can report on anything."

Discussing the newspaper's year-long coverage of a Cuban couple who had fled from Cuba to Albuquerque and ended up staying at Joy Junction, the reporter stated, "I ... think that by covering them for a year, you can write a story about making the transition from not only being homeless and country-less to being a productive member of society. I would wager that most of the homeless people who complain about the media are people who are not taking advantage of every possible opportunity to get off of the welfare rolls, and I think maybe there is a little bit of jealousy on their part, when they see somebody else doing what they talk about but never actually do."

Relating his doubts about how well-informed the homeless are about what the media do, this reporter stated, "Unless they're staying at a place like Joy Junction, where they have access to a television set from time to time, I'd wager that most of them are not going to spend 50¢ on a newspaper. I would wager that most of them do not really know what the problem is of the homeless in general. Homelessness to them is how it affects them personally, so while they're criticizing the media for not looking at them and for their own individual, particular circumstances, I think they're pretty much guilty of the same thing." He continued, "I would wager that most of those people who are homeless do not themselves have a handle on how big the problem is, and how multi-faceted it is, and I would also wager that the longer they are in that cycle of homelessness, the more it becomes about them. Period."

Albuquerque Print Reporter Number 2 (personal communication, February 18, 2004). A former reporter for The Albuquerque Tribune agreed that reporters should never be advocates. "Reporters are to report the facts," she wrote in an e-mail. "Sometimes the facts show homeless in a negative light. But those problems shouldn't fall on the shoulders of the reporters, but rather those in charge of the community."

She said that as a reporter for *The Tribune*, she covered the homeless in many different aspects. "I know that my editors want fair stories. And in my stories, I've tried to include the actual plight of the homeless person." Giving an example, she said, "After the Bosque fires and homeless were being run out of there, I interviewed a homeless man who had lived in the Bosque for 10 years. He gave us an inside look at what living free in the Bosque was like. When the city wanted to do a 'crack-down' on Central Avenue to rid small motels of people residing there for long periods of time, our paper wanted to know how that would affect the many homeless that lived in those motels."

She said her paper even covered the march to remember fallen homeless. "I can honestly say," she said, "I have made an effort to show how homelessness affects a person. I think my paper has supported my effort in doing that."

While praising her former paper, she had a different opinion about other Albuquerque media. "Homeless stories on the news and in the (Albuquerque) *Journal* are few and far between unless something bad happens regarding them," she said. "But that's only my opinion. And that doesn't apply to The Trib."

Overall, the findings here demonstrate from three perspectives, that coverage by the media of the culture of homelessness as a socio-political issue is incomplete and thus inaccurate. Therefore media coverage, which educates the general population, in this instance results in the homeless being portrayed in a potentially negative fashion.

In analyzing each segment of the research, I found a broadly negative assessment of media coverage of the issue of homelessness and of the homeless. First, the interview with a broadly knowledgeable source who works with 294 providers of services for the homeless across the country confirmed my anecdotal observations that the national media provide only limited coverage of homeless issues and they almost never do so to the depth necessary to provide their audiences with a substantial understanding of the issue of homelessness. Similarly, that person confirmed that while local media organizations around the country often do a better job than the national media of covering the phenomenon of homelessness, their coverage is nonetheless shallow and is usually a response to a local event, such as some violation of the law by a homeless person – again a negative portrayal of the homeless.

The research among the homeless themselves shows a certain expectation that the media should be interested in and sympathetic to the plight of the homeless. There was an additional expectation that members of the media needed to spend time with the homeless in order to adequately understand their perceived plight, and what sorts of support from a local community would be necessary to help them overcome their situation.

Finally, the interviews with people who work in the media indicate they are not particularly concerned about the phenomenon of homelessness or even of the homeless themselves, any more than they are any other segment of their local community. They found the expectation of the homeless that people who work in the media should spend time with the homeless in order to learn about them almost amusing. Members of the media said they feel no greater responsibility to understand or cover the homeless than they do any other community group.

5

Analytical Overview of the Interviews

My analysis of the interviews among both groups (the homeless and the media) suggest that there is a huge disconnect between what the homeless expect from the media and what people working in the media – both broadcast and print – choose to report in covering the homeless. When they make choices, editors in the media are commonly guided by their need to maintain their audiences, therefore their coverage must seem to them to be potentially interesting to their multiple publics.

For instance, a common thread running through interviews with the homeless is that people in the media would benefit from a more direct, first-hand encounter of the experience called "homelessness" by spending time with the homeless and getting to know them better. There seemed to be an implicit assumption by the homeless that the media exist to act as their advocates, an assumption that runs completely contrary to American journalistic principles. On the other hand, reporters pride themselves on being advocates for no one.

As one reporter said, there is a "fine line between being responsible for telling stories and being advocates for telling stories. My job is to be responsible in telling the stories."

In compiling this section it was necessary to maintain the anonymity of each individual by refraining from describing in any detail their specific situation and circumstances, though they represent a purposive sampling of the homeless culture. Each individual quoted has a diverse and powerful authentication although that will not be evident here.

However, one homeless respondent (No. 25) obviously had a very incongruent view of what the media should do. He said that reporters need to "find out if we need medical (care). Find out what kind of education we need to get out of this mess. Find out if the state can help us get a home. We're a minority. Nobody wants to look at us, out of sight, out of mind, like I say. Nobody wants to see us. We're a thorn in their side, actually."

Another respondent (No. 29) agreed, saying the media "should get in there.

Be one of us. Go to a shelter, stay there; see what it's like, what it feels like." This respondent was unaware that a reporter from the CBS affiliate in Albuquerque, New Mexico had done that, about six months prior to the interview.

The idea of spending time with the homeless did not go down well with one broadcast journalist in Albuquerque. That individual said, "There's no way in a million years I'm going to spend three days sitting around the campfire getting to know these people. And I hate to say it, but I don't know if our average viewer cares. I think people truly would tune out if they saw the life of a homeless person. You know what, I don't care. I think the attitude is, get a job, get some help, go to Joy Junction, whatever you need to do to get your services to get yourself back on the street. So I don't feel obligated to these people. Most of the time I don't care about their story, unless there's something positive coming out of a facility that's trying to help somebody ... but I'm looking for something positive in that yucky negative situation. In general, I don't think people care ... about the homeless."

As one broadcast journalist mentioned in an interview, homelessness is not "sexy." She added, "What's new? It's the same story we've been doing 10 years ago when we followed the homeless people, so I think that's one reason we don't cover it. How does it affect people is another reason. We always look for stories that affect people, and sometimes they don't. Sometimes they're crime stories that don't affect anybody and they're just quirky or interesting." Homelessness, the reporter said, "doesn't affect many people, and I say that with a grain of salt, because I know homelessness is a big problem that I think we all need to work on."

In terms of symbolic language, the view of this reporter that her life and the lives of her audience are not related to the lives of the homeless reflects a sense of social and psychological distance. The reporter cannot identify with the plight of homeless people. She is engaging in a certain amount of analysis, and her analytical conclusion is that she and her audience do not function in the same social sphere as the homeless, therefore she and the audience she is seeking to reach don't need or want to know much about homeless people or the phenomenon of homelessness.

Viewers see the issue of homelessness "selfishly," the reporter said. "That homeless person doesn't affect me, doesn't come in contact with me,' they say, and they won't care as viewers, and that's why we don't cover the homeless people."

Identifying or sensing absolutely no obligation to cover the homeless, this reporter said, "I know some people have gotten some bad breaks, and I know they're on the streets because of a number of reasons, ... a lot of times for mental reasons, and I don't feel one bit sorry for those people. I refuse to give them money on the street corners. I will donate to a shelter like Joy Junction, but I refuse to help these people on the street because my perception is that they're going to be buying booze or drugs (and) not ... doing anything good with it."

This reporter said that the hostility exhibited by some of the homeless toward the media further serves to exacerbate the difficulty of coverage. "When there's a story about panhandling (and) ... we go either to try to get video of people just trying to get a few extra dollars on the streets, or shooting video of homeless people, they are very hostile. (They say), 'Get that camera away from me. I want nothing to do with you.' We say, 'Well, talk to us about your situation and why it works for you' and they don't even want to talk to you. As soon as they see you, they get this instant attitude, (saying), 'Get the hell away from me, you guys are all bad.'"

However, a photojournalist for an Albuquerque network news affiliate had a different answer that may add another perspective to the issue. He said, "I think the media covers the homeless the way we cover a lot of things ... we focus on the negative in everything. I think the news is kinda negative and people have asked for that, when you do ratings surveys, when they asked the public. When you have too many features and you go too soft, people don't watch your (news) show."

This puts the media in the delicate position of having to play a balancing game, presenting substantive community issues in a serious way that may not be entertaining enough to draw an audience, or abandoning serious presentation of content in favor of being more entertaining. Any sober analysis must recognize that television news is presented to viewers in the context of an entertainment medium. As a grandson of media baron William Randolph Hearst once said, "Television is an entertainment medium with bits of information thrown in, and newspapers are an information medium with bits of entertainment thrown in like the raisins in cereal."

The interviews with homeless people reflected that they were completely unaware of the constraints of commercial television news, which lives or dies depending on its ratings position in the particular market it occupies. Bearing these attitudes in mind when the homeless complain about the media's coverage of homelessness, at least as far as broadcast news goes, there appear to be two options. A homeless respondent (No. 29) suggested one approach. She said that better communication is needed between the media and the homeless.

That would be a start; however, it seems that the only way to achieve a substantive difference in the way the homeless are currently portrayed is to change the system. Even the highest paid employees of the broadcast networks and their affiliates are victims of a ratings system that governs what will or will not make it on the air. Controversy, drama and criminal activity are the three legs upon which broadcast news stands. There are two well-known axioms in television news: "If it's sleazy, it's easy," meaning the story is easy to do, and "If it bleeds, it leads," meaning that stories about death and injury are especially interesting and should go to the top of the newscast. The print media have their own idiosyncrasies. In the sample of stories studied for the research for this book, newspapers much more often went beyond merely covering the homeless to cover the phenomenon of homelessness while television focused on homeless people who are the observable manifestation of homelessness, but a manifestation with a certain social stigma attached. However, newspapers usually did not talk to real homeless people, opting instead to speak to people who organize and provide services for the homeless – essentially voices of the homeless without the social stigma of homelessness. There was much more coverage of crimes by or against the homeless on the broadcast networks than there were stories that focused on the issue of homelessness. This issue will be dealt with in greater depth in the general analysis section.

6

Entertainment-Education Theory / Biblical Theory

Entertainment-Education Theory

My research primarily uses the theoretical grids of Everett Rogers and Jayakumar Christian through which to analyze its findings. The agenda-setting theory expanded and popularized by Everett Rogers and first coined by Bernard Cohen (1963) says, "The media aren't always successful at telling us what to think, but they are quite successful at telling us what to think about."

The term "agenda-setting" was first used in a study by Maxwell E. McCombs and Donald L. Shaw (McCombs & Shaw, 1972), although they were not the first to look at this issue. In the study, the researchers interviewed 100 undecided voters in Chapel Hill, North Carolina and asked them what issues they were most concerned about in the coming (1968) election. After they worked out the issues deemed most important by the voters, the researchers evaluated the media serving Chapel Hill (both print and broadcast) for the content of their stories. McCombs and Shaw found an almost perfect correlation between the types of stories that were covered most often and the voters' concern for the same issues. Studies have shown that the number of times a story is repeated in the news will affect peoples' perception of the story's importance, regardless of what is said about the topic.

The authors noted (ix) that they identified three main components of the agenda-setting process: a) the media agenda, b) the public agenda, and c) the policy agenda. This research on the way the media portrays the homeless only deals with the media agenda.

Dearing and Rogers noted some generalizations about the agenda-setting process. They include that a) during different time frames, different media place varying degrees of importance on certain issues, b) the events occurring in the world (also known as real world indicators) are not terribly important in determining the media agenda, c) the White House, the *New York Times* and "trigger events" such as the recent tsunami disaster play an important role in seeing an issue placed on the media agenda, d) the results of scientific research do not play an important role in the agenda-setting process, and e) the position of an issue on the media agenda helps determine the issue's relevance on the public agenda (Dearing & Rogers, 1996, pp. 90–92). In addition, the research also draws on the theory of entertainment-education. In their 1999 book, *Entertainment-Education: A Communication Strategy for Social Change*, authors Everett Rogers and Arvind Singhal also showed how public opinion can be formed by the media though this time intentionally. As the book's cover reads, in their assessment of entertainment-education the authors look at the process of (intentionally) designing and implementing media messages to both entertain and educate, for the purpose of increasing an audience's knowledge about an educational issue, creating favorable attitudes and changing overt behavior."

While there are effective results and substantive behavioral change arising out of deliberate entertainment-projects, there is just as much perceptual and attitudinal change occurring unintentionally from the so-called "news" which is in actuality entertainment masquerading as news.

Simplemente Maria

A graphic portrayal of the power of media effects upon the public perception of a social issue was seen in the events associated with the showing of the wildly successful Peruvian soap opera "Simplemente Maria." In the drama, Maria, a former Peruvian maid who wanted to better herself, was attending adult literacy classes for neighborhood maids. When she gave birth to her son, she was fired by her employers.

Maria's literacy teacher's mother showed her how to sew, and she worked as a seamstress in a local dress shop where she used a Singer sewing machine. Maria ended up launching her own fashion business. She ultimately became a very successful fashion designer, moved into a big mansion and emigrated to Paris where she directed her own fashion empire.

While the series was originally produced just to be successful, no one could have foreseen its unintended educational effect. In countries where

"Simplemente Maria" was broadcast, housemaids began to sew and there was a dramatic increase in enrollment in sewing classes and adult literacy classes. There was also an upsurge in the sales of Singer sewing machines (Singhal & Rogers, 1999, p. 45).

Although the research on "Simplemente Maria" was "fragmentary and anecdotal," because there was no scholarly research conducted on the audience effects of the soap opera (Singhal & Rogers, 1999), any doubts about the powerful effects of the media should have been alleviated by what was learned from the theory of entertainment-education.

"Simplemente Maria" had a huge role in the formulation of the theoretically-based entertainment education strategy, the concept of consciously combining entertainment and educational media content (Singhal & Rogers, 1999, p. 45).

Using as a theoretical backdrop, the unintended educational effects of "Simplemente Maria" that were shown anecdotally and the intentional effects of the entertainment-education strategy and agenda-setting theory that have been demonstrated through social scientific research, the continuous use of the word "homeless" in a primarily negative manner for a small number of homeless people involved in situations that generate a lot media attention may tend to result in viewers thinking negatively about all of the homeless with whom they come into contact.

The results of a 1999 study (Anastasio, Rose, & Chapman, 1999), using a social identity approach, asked whether the media can create public opinion concluded that could be the case. The study's abstract read in part,

> The media remains a powerful presence in U.S. culture. It gives people news of world and local events, it entertains, and it may even function as a companion to children. Because it functions as a window to the outside world, what appears across its landscape actually may become people's reality. Thus, the potential for distorting their view of that world is high if the picture provided is unrepresentative of actual events. For example, the prevalence of violent acts on television has been linked to increased aggression and escalating impressions of a dangerous world, and the overrepresentation of youth and beauty may be a causal factor of

eating disorders. In this article, we explore the possibility that the media may also serve as a powerful creator of the very public opinions it seeks to reflect in its news. Subtle nonverbal cues of newscasters have been shown to influence voting behavior, and the media's overrepresentation of the proportion of blacks in poverty may decrease whites' support of welfare. By portraying a world in which people's opinions are based on their ethnic or demographic group membership, the media may also subtly but powerfully create the very opinions they seek to reflect (Anastasio, Rose & Chapman, 1999).

Biblical Theory

Dealing with such disparate groups as the homeless and the media, it was hard to fit either into the theory proposed by Jayakumar Christian. In his book, *God of the Empty Handed: Poverty, Power and the Kingdom of God*, Christian explored the relationship of poverty and powerlessness, using an integrated approach of anthropology, sociology, politics and theology.

Christian analyzed some secular development theories as well as evangelical, Dalit and liberation theologies and he assessed some traditional historical responses to poverty. Looking at the real meaning of powerlessness, he described some of the many challenges facing the Christian church today, and provided an alternative response that he believed explores the concept of power according to the theology of the kingdom of God. Christian's proposition is that people who deal with the poor need to be authentic, that their response to the poor must not only focus on persons and relationships, but must also be more than just a planned programmatic response (Christian, 1999, p. 220).

However, many of the homeless have no idea of or desire for any concept of Biblical truth and that same fact also applies to many journalists who provide coverage about the homeless. In this study, the only media coverage of the homeless that would be assessed as approximating a focus on "persons and relationships" are those stories in this study that deal with the issue of homelessness. However, because of the structure of the media industries, even those stories are oriented more toward ratings than toward relationships.

In a recent issue of an Albuquerque newsweekly (*Crosswinds Weekly*, February 24 – March 3, 2004), a column by the magazine's publisher dealt with what he called "Body Bag Journalism." Author Steve Lawrence wrote,

> Watch the first ten minutes of your local TV newscast, on any given night, and you get body bags. And weather ... The killings are generally senseless ... Do we learn anything new from these stories? Do we learn anything essential? Do we understand crime, violence and their causes any better? Do we learn anything important about our community? Do we learn how to avoid violence? Do we learn how to stop these killings? The answer to all of the above: no ... (But) TV news people ... remind you that violence drives ratings. In other words, they will say, we are only giving the public what it wants. This, as has been said before, is the 'drug pusher' standard for news judgment. As a reporter or editor you don't tell people the stories they need to know, or should know. You give them what they want, like dope or alcohol.

Christian would agree with Lawrence's column. Unfortunately, neither is financially viable in America, with the current system of journalism being supported by advertising.

There is no "kingdom based response," as Christian put it, when it comes to dealing with the poor (Christian, 1999, pp. 220–221). Neither is there a Biblical understanding by the secular media of how God deals with the poor. To do even a part of what Christian proposes would require a total restructuring of American commercial journalism with its commercially oriented ratings system. It would also, in effect, turn journalists from reporters into advocates for the homeless, something that the homeless interviewed for this study apparently wanted, but that reporters indignantly insisted they would never be.

However, Christian also suggests (1999, p. 221) that poverty practitioners must be equipped with the skills to analyze the worldview of a people as a necessary part of poverty analysis. No matter how helpful that would be, the homeless generally have no understanding of the role of the media, and members of the press also generally have no understanding of why people are or become homeless. That is not to say they should sympathize with the reasons given by the homeless, but perhaps better stories would be written if journalists understood at least something of the world-view and mindset of the people about whom they are writing.

A major obstacle to this is the role of the general assignment (GA) reporter, who is constantly called upon to be an "overnight expert." For example: A GA reporter arrives at work and is assigned to cover a story dealing with a situation, industry or organization with which he or she has little or no knowledge or experience. Often a reporter will read background information about the issue while on the way to the scene of the story. Therefore, if this is a broadcast journalist functioning as a general assignment reporter, not only does he or she not know a lot about the issue to be reported on, but usually has little time available to create the story. Consequently, it is going to be practically impossible for the reporter to acquire any sort of familiarity with the homeless and their worldview and put a situation into perspective.

This issue does not seem to be as much of a problem with the print media as it is with the broadcast media. In most instances, print media seem to have a "beat" reporter assigned to cover stories dealing with the homeless. Being assigned a beat allows a level of familiarity with an issue or organization that a GA reporter does not have.

Christian concluded his proposed plan by saying that kingdom power should cause "ripples of transformation," as it "equips the poor to be agents of transformation and thus initiate movements" (Christian, 1999, p. 221) and that a kingdom-based response affirms that power belongs to the Lord. "That means that those people who deal with the poor on a grassroots level must live their lives in a manner that affirms this statement. There will be a positive consequence for doing that," he commented, continuing, "This will enable the poor to perceive the link between power as expressed in a kingdom-based response and dependence of the community of practitioners on Jesus Christ, to whom all power and glory belongs" (Christian, 1999, p. 221).

Christian's wish for people, "That means that those people who deal with the poor on a grassroots level must live their lives in a manner that affirms this statement" corresponded with the often expressed complaint by the homeless that reporters need to come and hang out with them around the camp fire.

Another author expressed a wish similar to Christian's in his book *God in the Alley*. Greg Paul wrote, "I came to the conclusion that I needed to be in a place where I would have to submit to the direction of gay and lesbian people, where I would be accountable to them for my attitudes and actions, and could learn something from their culture. In short, I would try to be *among* them, instead of trying to reach them from outside. In fact, I needed to move away from thinking about 'them' and learn to think about 'us'" (2004, p. 12).

The fact of the culture of homelessness being more than just needing a place to stay was also borne out in the interviews conducted with guests staying at Joy Junction and other homeless individuals. Many of those had the attitude that the poor treatment they felt they were experiencing at the hands of the media was not their own fault, and that if people in the media were to spend time with them, the media would perceive them in a more positive fashion.

However, it would be helpful for reporters regularly assigned to the homeless to do observation of this nature, because it would help them place future situations in better perspective. They would no longer be the "overnight expert" referred to in the results and analysis section of this research. In addition, if observation of this nature were to be standard operating procedure for all reporters (both print and broadcast) prior to covering the homeless, perhaps reporters would be able to produce more effective stories on the homeless without being advocates.

While not trying to turn reporters into "poverty practitioners," Christian's suggestion (1999, p. 221) that poverty practitioners do need to be equipped with the skills to analyze the world-view of a people as a necessary part of poverty analysis is appropriate. Such training would help reporters acquire some of those skills. In addition, it should go far toward helping to break down the serious disconnect that currently exists between the homeless and the media. Such training should go far toward helping break down the serious disconnect that currently exists between the media and the homeless.

7

Analysis

Research Question

The overarching question this research seeks to answer is straightforward: How do the mass media represent the homeless to the larger society or mainstream society?

In this study, I take the "larger society" and "mainstream society" to mean people who have no experience with being homeless or significant personal association with people who are homeless. This question arises from concern that the national media present an inaccurate picture of America's homeless as otherwise ordinary people whose problems can be "fixed" by a meal and some overnight shelter.

This research question was derived from an understanding of sympathetic media coverage portraying the homeless as being ordinary people whose issues were a result of unfortunate societal influences. For example,

> An analysis of the television news media between 1982 and 1988 concluded that most portrayals did not stigmatize the homeless and, when the causes of homelessness were mentioned, they tended to center on societal factors. Likewise, in analyzing stories from national evening television newscasts and national magazines from 1986 to 1989, the Center for Media and Public Affairs found that coverage tended to be sympathetic, with the majority of stories focusing on local programs and services or on descriptions of homeless people instead of on the causes of homelessness. The stereotypic image of the unemployed male alcoholic was rare, with images focusing on families and children as frequently as single males. When causes were referred to, they were more likely to focus on structural causes such as housing market forces instead of personal problems. Almost 70% of the portrayals of public reactions to the homeless were characterized as compassionate in nature. (Buck & Toro, 2002, p. 3)

I attempted to consider this question from multiple perspectives, producing a set of three related research questions:

Question 1   How do the major news media represent the homeless in news stories about homeless people and homelessness?

Question 2   How do homeless people perceive that they are represented in the mass media?

Question 3   How do news reporters and anchors perceive their responsibility to cover the homeless and homelessness as a cultural phenomenon in modern America?

Analysis Overview

The media coverage stories studied for this project show that, by a ratio of approximately 2:1, the print media focused much more on the issue of homelessness than did the broadcast media.

However, many of the print articles dealing with the issues of homelessness did not feature any comment from a homeless person. Often these stories failed to show a complete picture, and character portrayals of the homeless, when they were presented, were sketchy at best.

Conversely the broadcast media focused much more on crimes committed by or against the homeless. There are potentially serious results that can be inferred from this type of coverage. At a minimum, Americans who rely on the media as a major source of continuing education about the social worlds around them, will go away from the media coverage ill-informed about homelessness as a social phenomenon. Further, mainstream Americans will receive an incomplete, and therefore flawed, picture of the people who are homeless, which may lead them to trivialize the homeless and their plight.

While there are unintended consequences of media coverage, it can be seen clearly from real-life cases that the media can have dramatic impact – even when no such outcome is intended. One useful illustration is the case of the hugely successful Peruvian soap opera "Simplemente Maria" (Singhal & Rogers, 1999, p. 41), when an overwhelming number of viewers responded to the concepts presented in the drama. We find other illustrations of media impact in the scientifically measured effects of agenda-setting and entertainment-education.

Because news stories studied for this project often used the word homeless in a negative way, one may assume that, after seeing the homeless and their subculture being portrayed this way so many times, the average viewer may unconsciously form a negative picture of the homeless because he or she is being informally educated to do so. This is not to suggest that the news media intentionally presented the homeless in a particular fashion. Rather, the interviews with a modest-sized theoretical sample of journalists indicate they have no intention of maligning or disparaging the homeless. However, they largely are ignorant of the day-to-day lives of the homeless, and they have no interest in being further educated about this cultural phenomenon.

In addition, the issue of homelessness is not a priority on the media agenda because it does not provide the requisite ratings boost. This is based upon the theory of agenda-setting and interviews with local media personnel.

The fact that three major stories featuring the word "homeless" (and these stories receiving much media attention), while informally educating media consumers to think negatively about the homeless, is incidental in one sense. The major players in the story could have as easily been priests or firemen, and they would have received the same negative treatment. As several reporters stated in a variety of ways, "We are uniformly negative. We just don't pick on the homeless."

However, even if this self-assessment is true and journalists approach their coverage of lawyers, firefighters, police officers, accountants and others on the basis of a uniformly negative *weltanschauung*, the homeless are likely to suffer more from such an approach than members of other groups, including members of certain occupations and professions. This is because the homeless have fewer resources to use in challenging the portrayal of their cultural status than do other members of society.

The results of my research indicate that the homeless are "extensively stigmatized" in broadcast news and information programs. While this research found that stories concerning the homeless and criminal activity predominated, Lind and Danowski (1999) found that the homeless were commonly presented as mentally ill, substance abusers, often involved in criminal behavior, often in poor health and often suffering from contagious diseases. "The stigmatized image of the homeless that the audience receives is not countered by an alternative image encouraging sympathy and support" (as cited in Min, 1999, p. 118).

However, this study indicated that the electronic media did not really deal with the causes of homelessness (as cited in Min, 1999, p. 118) in stories about crimes committed by or against the homeless.

This research found that the print media had a substantially higher percentage of stories about the phenomenon of homelessness than did the broadcast sources. However, very few of the print articles focused upon homeless people in a way that indicated reporters actually interviewed them, got to know them and saw how a combination of personal problems and governmental policies affect them in their daily life.

Despite the reporters' positions on this question, from an ethnographic and social scientific standpoint, getting to know the homeless likely would, in fact, be helpful, as it would give reporters more of a feel for the individuals about whom they were writing. It might also help to identify discernible, representative and inferable traits of a homeless population over a given time. This is surely invaluable in effective reporting, as opposed to writing about a possibly unrepresentative snapshot of a few homeless people on one or two nights.

In addition, many of the print articles that actually dealt with the issue of "homelessness," as opposed to just including the word "homeless," did not feature comments from a homeless person. For example, articles or transcripts on the work of homeless shelters might feature comments from shelter officials about the people they work with, but then failed to include comments from homeless people. Other articles featured politicians talking about budget cuts and their consequences for the homeless or activists ruminating about the same issue, but the writers of these articles did not speak to homeless people who would be directly affected by the budget cuts.

While it could be debated whether the homeless need to be featured prominently in media stories dealing with the issue of homelessness, it would appear that some type of comment from the homeless would have been helpful in these articles. Ultimately, they are the people most affected, and without their existence, there would have been no story.

Regarding the homeless not being featured in media accounts of their plight, I personally experienced this phenomenon while working on this book.

After some bitterly cold days and nights when the temperature in New Mexico was colder than that in Minnesota, my cell phone rang one morning just after four o'clock in December, 2004. It was one of the staff members at Joy Junction, saying he had just received a call from a local network news affiliate asking if a reporter and photographer could come down to Joy Junction at 5 a.m. to talk about how the cold weather was affecting the homeless.

Knowing that this would be very positive, I appeared in five brief news segments at 5 a.m., 5.30 a.m., 6 a.m., 6.30 a.m. and 7.25 a.m. The first two segments were taped outside Joy Junction's main building, and the last three were shot inside the shelter kitchen. Food being prepared and individuals being fed were prominently featured in two of the last three segments. If those segments had been analyzed for the purposes of this research, they would have been classified as stories that dealt not with the plight of one or even a few homeless people, but with the issue of homelessness: in this case, how the cold weather affected the homeless as a group or class of people.

The reporter asked me to provide an on-air description of what he felt it was like for the homeless to be outside in the bone-chilling cold. While willing to oblige, I was never asked if he could find a homeless person willing to speak on camera about being outside in such cold conditions. A homeless person would have been more effective at describing that experience because he or she would have endured that hardship. Therefore the most important ingredient in a story about the homeless was missing – the homeless!

While it would be easy to criticize such coverage, before doing so it is important to consider possible reasons for not asking the homeless to appear on those news segments. The reasons could include lack of time and the challenge of finding a homeless person who was willing to speak on camera, as well as being sufficiently presentable and articulate to satisfy the expectations of a television reporter or producer in the field location. Those variables differ from one reporter or producer to another and from station to station.

While the homeless were admittedly profiled in some of the stories analyzed, one reader who scored the news stories took issue with a number of them. She liked stories dealing with people overcoming the obstacles of homelessness to attain success (such as "Homeless to Harvard"), but she also considered them problematic: "These stories are meant to shine light on the determination of the human spirit and what it can accomplish in even the worst of circumstances," she wrote. "Overall, I like these stories ... (but) I also find them dangerous because they very seldom tell about all the help, hard work and knock downs or setbacks encountered along the way. But how much can you say in a 500 words or less story?"

She noted that when the actual issue of homelessness was addressed, the tone taken was often that the homeless were victims. "The background of why the person or persons are homeless is written sketchily at best and most often gives little accountability to the homeless for their plight or actually any accountability to any reason at all. It's ... usually just assumed that it's due to the social ills of our time."

There may be a number of reasons for the "sketchy" writing. One might be that because the homeless, as a rule, are notoriously reticent to discuss their plight in depth, the reporter really has no choice but to provide a limited portrayal. But if the reporter were more familiar with the homeless, then presumably more effective questions could be asked, which could lead to more complete answers and a better story.

A Reporter's World View Guides the Questions

However, a journalistic willingness or unwillingness to hold the homeless accountable for their plight may also influence the type of questions asked and could depend on a reporter's "world view." As researcher Marvin Olasky wrote in *Central Ideas in the Development of American Journalism: A Narrative History,*

> Essentially, world views are clusters of convictions and values not verifiable by the means of natural science. Every person, whether religious or atheistic, has a world view ... When psychologist B.

F. Skinner says that human beings are made solely of matter and
we think with our bodies because bodies are all we are, we need
to ask how he learned that. The answer he gives will have nothing
at all to do with science; it is as much a matter of faith as anything
Jerry Falwell says (1991, p. 144).

Essentially concurring with Olasky, Reader One added, "I'm not sure where
I stand on how the media portray the homeless. As in any case, I'm sure
that there are ratings to be (considered). After all, it's a business. Some
reporters are better than others; some are more socially minded and feel that
we are our brother's keeper. In the end, I think that the bias of each individual
goes into the reporting and the reading, hearing, or watching of reports about
the homeless and therefore, colored the opinion."

Analysis of Stories of the Homeless and Crime

As I noted earlier, the articles dealing with a criminal action committed by
or against a person identified as homeless comprised more than 15% of the
total stories read. The remaining stories in this category dealt mainly with
a variety of violent assaults committed on or by homeless people. The
majority of the stories were about a) Elizabeth Smart's kidnapping, b) the
East Coast snipers, and c) the Chante Mallard story. In the Smart kidnapping,
her alleged abductor was regularly referred to as homeless. In the D.C. sniper
case, much was made of the two alleged gunmen having stayed in a homeless
shelter. The Mallard case dealt with a crime committed against a homeless
person. Mallard was the Dallas woman who let a homeless man die after
he was impaled in her windshield; she made no serious effort to remove
him and did not call for assistance from the emergency services. She is now
serving a life sentence in prison.

Reader One said that much was made of the fact that Mallard's victim
was "homeless." "All the gory details were in there about him being left to
die in the car windshield and then dismembered and left in the park," she
wrote, "but in every story they mentioned over and over that he was homeless.
My question would be – would they mention that I was not homeless, or
some other socially significant thing about me?"

The print media collectively averaged half the number of stories dealing with crimes committed by or against the homeless, while the broadcast media averaged twice the total number of stories dealing with such crimes. The broadcast sources had about five times more stories dealing with crimes committed by or against the homeless than the print sources. Fox News had the highest percentage of those, with over 40 percent of its stories dealing with crime.

Violence in General on Television

From a broader perspective, I inferred from the data that the broadcast media tend to focus on the stories dealing with crimes committed by or against the homeless, because they are violent, sensational and feature conflict – a staple of both successful drama in general and of successful television in particular. While violence sells on television, this refers to all violence, not just crimes committed by the homeless or any other group. There were almost as many stories that dealt with crimes committed against a homeless person as by a homeless person.

It is not that the media only cover the homeless when they do something wrong. It is that for the most part the media only cover anything when there is something wrong, new, exceptional and out of the ordinary. This fact is not something the homeless being interviewed understood. They failed to see the general uniform negativity of the media about everything and everyone they cover.

In most cases, anything cheerful is relegated to the end of the newscast and is only a few seconds long, known as a "kicker." This is a short, lighthearted story used to end the broadcast, and intended to leave the viewer with a good feeling after having watched a newscast filled with crime, death, destruction and other kinds of stories that are less than uplifting.

Negativity and the Homeless

However, there is a potential problem when there is so much negativity in broadcast news associated with the word homeless. For example, the stories that Fox News focused on were those dealing with crimes committed by or against the homeless, a) the D.C. snipers case where the alleged shooters stayed in a homeless shelter, b) the Laci Peterson case (because prior to her murder she apparently walked in a park frequented by the homeless), c) the Chante Mallard case that involved a homeless man who was run over and impaled through the windshield of a car by a driver who was suffering the effects of drugs and alcohol, and d) the Elizabeth Smart kidnapping. The stories dealing with the Smart kidnapping mostly identified her alleged kidnapper as being a homeless wanderer, a self-proclaimed prophet or a variety of other names all containing the word "homeless."

A major question for me as I was doing the research for this book was whether this coverage of acts perpetrated by or against the homeless (as opposed to reporting that deals with the issue of homelessness) educates and influences public perception of the homeless.

Linking the Word "Homeless" with Criminal Activity

In an Oct. 27, 2002 program on CNN dealing with the D.C. snipers, a guest on the show said, in reference to the publicity generated by the situation, "We had very good reason to believe that in general this saturation publicity creates a market for mass murder, a climate for additional serial spree."

While my research did not test for the effects of the media upon its consumers, other research in the field of entertainment-education and agenda-setting has done so. Based upon those scientific theories and the impact of "Simplemente Maria," it is reasonable to infer that the linking of the word homeless with criminal activity is educating viewers to think of the homeless as criminals.

In the same CNN report, another guest was asked when he analyzed the coverage of the D.C. snipers, whether or not the reporting, which was replete with logos and theme music, was "marketing murder or serving a public need." He replied that it was both.

Therefore with the word "homeless" being mentioned so much in conjunction with criminal activity, it is reasonable to assume that while these stories are serving a so-called public need, the result of so many of them dealing with crimes committed by or against the homeless is that they are marketing murder and informally educating the viewing audience into accepting a very negative image of the homeless and the culture of homelessness. For example, a message about the danger posed by the homeless was articulated on a March 12, 2003, edition of CNN's "Larry King Show." Participant Marc Klaas said in a panel discussion on the Elizabeth Smart kidnapping case,

> We have to pull lessons out of these stories. Now, earlier last year when all of the children were disappearing, a family in St. Louis brought a homeless man into their home. He murdered a little girl. The Smarts have this bizarre habit of bringing criminals and homeless guys into their home. As a result of that they lost their daughter for nine months. So, I think the lesson here is, 'don't bring a homeless guy home.' I want to show (compassion) toward the homeless, give them $40 and send them to a hotel, but don't take them home. (Klass, CNN, 2003)

Although stories dealing with crimes committed by or against the homeless frequently mention the word "homeless," they do not usually contribute toward our understanding of the issue of homelessness. As has been noted, during the coverage of the D.C. snipers and the Elizabeth Smart cases, the word "homeless" was liberally associated with both situations. For example, the Smart kidnapper was often described as a self-proclaimed "homeless prophet," while the snipers were frequently described as having stayed in a homeless shelter. Reader One suggested that such a linkage results in homeless shelters being portrayed as "havens for criminals."

Further study is needed to see exactly what such association eventually does in the specific instance of linking the word homeless with criminal activity. However, based upon the academic literature, it seems reasonable to infer that by focusing on a few high profile cases that happened to involve the homeless, the viewing public is being educated to regard the homeless as criminals.

8

Conclusion and Recommendations

The print media I studied portrayed the issue of homelessness in a more favorable light than did the broadcast media, which in its focus, tended to depict the homeless as part of the criminal element. However, a post-election survey by the nonpartisan Pew Research Center for the People and the Press that dealt in part with voters' thoughts on Campaign 2004 and the importance of moral values in the 2004 election, showed that television far surpasses newspapers as a primary source of information for the average American (Pew Research Center, 2004).

This information was the answer to survey question 26, which asked, "How did you get most of your news about the presidential election campaign? From television, from newspapers, from radio, from magazines, or from the Internet?"

The following analysis refers to the fact that the television media were the primary source of information for news during the November 1992, 1996 and 2000 presidential elections. Therefore, I contend that this form of media impact and consequently informally educate, concerning issues which are portrayed to the general viewing population.

Table 4. Survey Question No. 26: "How Did You Get Most of Your News about the Presidential Election Campaign? From Television, from Newspapers, from Radio, from Magazines, or from the Internet?" (From Pew Research Center, 2004)

		Nov. 2000	Nov. 1996	Nov. 1992
76	Television	70	72	82
46	Newspapers	39	60	57
22	Radio	15	19	12
6	Magazines	4	11	9
21	Internet	11	3	–
2	Other	1	4	6
1	Don't know / Refused		4	6

While that survey did not deal with the type of media people turned to for news in general, a 2002 Pew survey, *"Public's News Habits Little Changed by September 11: Americans Lack Background to Follow International News,"* reported a significant decline in newspaper readership, saying, "People are increasingly turning away from newspapers." More specifically, the research found,

> Regular newspaper readership ... continues to inch downward. Just 41% of respondents say they read a paper the previous day, compared with 47% in 2000 and 48% in 1998. Since 1991, ... a large portion of this decline has occurred in the 35–49 age category. At the same time, it should be noted that older people have stuck with newspapers to a relatively greater degree than with network news" (Pew Research Center Study, 2002).

The survey report also noted that the network television news audience has decreased while the cable news audience has increased. However, the Pew survey found,

> the steady erosion of the regular audience for network evening news over the past decade has abated. Roughly one-third (32%) regularly watch one of the nightly network news broadcasts, compared with 30% in 2000. This is comparable to the overall cable news audience of 33%. Still, with the exception of CNBC, the viewer ship of major cable channels are up slightly since 2000, and the Fox News Channel's audience rivals CNN (22% regularly watch Fox, 25% CNN). (Pew Research Center Study, 2002)

The Pew study raises a question about the comparability of samples. The Newspaper Association of America reports in its publication, *Facts About Newspapers 2004*, that in 2004, 57% of men and 52% of women read a newspaper daily (and that number increased to 62% and 63% respectively for Sunday readership). The survey also found that newspaper readership increases with education, household income, job responsibility and home value. Consequently, these data suggest that those individuals who are or who may become decision makers in their community, state or even the nation are availing themselves of the continuing informal education that they perceive they need to be knowledgeable citizens and make better decisions.

Comparable information on the audiences of broadcast news is less readily available. Such data usually are only available in studies in individual broadcast markets. Broadcasters pay for those studies and usually limit the availability of data to station employees.

CNN's advantage over the Fox News Channel is clearly shown among middle-aged respondents. Fully 28% of those aged 40 to 65 watch CNN regularly, compared with 21% who are regular viewers of Fox. Fox is competitive with CNN among those in the younger and older age groups; 21% of those under age 40 watch Fox regularly and the same number watch CNN regularly. CNN leads Fox among senior citizens by only 27% to 24%. As a result, the median age of regular Fox viewers is slightly lower than that of CNN regulars (44 vs. 46), and both are significantly lower than the network evening news broadcasts (http://people-press.org/reports/display.php3?PageID'613).

The broadcast media studied in this book did not do a very thorough job of covering the issue of homelessness, especially in terms of concentrating on individuals who engage in attempting to explore possible methods of dealing with its causes and cures, choosing instead to focus on crimes committed by or against the homeless.

Based upon the academic literature and the interviews I conducted, continued coverage of this nature, (i.e., continually associating the word "homeless" with criminal acts) could lead media viewers and readers to conclude, however erroneously, that being homeless is tantamount to being a criminal. That is a significant change from the media's coverage of the homeless in the 1980's when the homeless were presented as individuals worthy of public sympathy, whose homelessness was not generally their own fault, but which represented one of society's endemic shortcomings.

Based upon interviews with local media professionals and the theory of agenda-setting, it is reasonable to infer that much of the sensationalistic coverage of stories dealing with crimes committed by or against the homeless is ratings driven. The issue of homelessness does not rank high on the media agenda because it is not, apparently, what consumers want to see.

Ratings are driven by stories involving high crimes and scandal, rather, than compassionate human stories whose outcome is noble and self-sacrificing, rather than tragic and compelling.

The role of the media seems to be focused on the abject truth of a particular, but not necessarily representative set of circumstances, rather than on the absolute truth. The danger in so doing is that the viewing audience could come to believe that isolated incidences, on which the media continues to focus, such as the Elizabeth Smart kidnapping, Laci Peterson murder, the Washington D.C. Snipers, referenced earlier in this research, is typical behavior of the group being portrayed. Thus, in connecting homelessness with criminal activity in this manner, the media, inadvertently in their efforts to gain significant ratings, point the viewer in a particular direction rather than presenting the facts and allowing the viewer to make his or her own decisions about the information being presented. This "information" is shaped by the media's proclivity toward sensationalism and scandal, both staples of American journalism, elements which the culture of homelessness and most news stories about the homeless lack.

Christian and Hiebert elaborate on the "world view" (Christian) and the "Western World View" (Hiebert) as it relates to the issue of "poverty" (Christian) and "materialism" (Hiebert), as being the framework which compels the decision-makers, i.e., those who possess the material wealth to effectuate change in this social dilemma. Who better to drive the "world view" and accomplish positive social change than the media? Yet, if the media continue to negatively influence the general viewing public by presenting sensational ratings-driven stories that portray the homeless as dangerous and intentionally criminal, the viewing public will possess an even more negative perception of the homeless than they already have. That perception could, quite possibly, result in a significant lack of compassion for the plight of the homeless, thus influencing the viewing public to hold the homeless in contempt, rather than inspiring them to reach out to those in need which would be the virtuous Christian ethos, as well as the viewpoint expressed by Jayakumar Christian.

However, because the print and broadcast media studied for this research are profit-driven businesses, they are forced to appeal to and satisfy the wishes of their audiences and advertisers.

Editor Steve Lawrence, in the Albuquerque newsweekly *Crosswinds Weekly*, commenting about the media's coverage of crime, said "The news is *why* crime happens. The news is how we can prevent crime and criminal behavior." Presumably this same writer would say about the homeless, "The news is *why* homelessness happens. The news is how we can prevent homelessness and homeless behavior." But as one local reporter said, that doesn't sell. Both broadcast media and print media are businesses that have to make a profit in order to survive. It is beyond the scope of this book to question the prevailing structure of American journalism, but the research here does show what image the media are presenting of the homeless and infers from entertainment-education research, the possible effects upon audiences of what is being presented.

While the coverage and concentration of the print media on the issue of homelessness is superior to that of the broadcast media, their effect and impact are much less than the broadcast media because of significantly smaller audiences.

There are different constraints on the broadcast and print media. Television news tends to be much more of a headline service focusing on capturing audience attention and does not usually have the time or the resources of the print media to extensively investigate or explore an issue or cause. Conversely, the print media can substantively explore in more depth and educate its audience regarding social issues.

There is little possibility of reporters getting to know the homeless in the manner expressed by Christian or Paul. Too many commercial constraints are placed on both print and broadcast media for that to be a viable reality.

A first step toward improving coverage of the issue of homelessness so that it comes closer to realizing Christian's proposal would be an increased level of communication between the media and the homeless.

Secondly, reporters need to educate themselves to better understand the issue. In addition, more beat (as opposed to general assignment) reporters should be assigned to cover homelessness. That likely would result in more appropriate contextualization of stories dealing with homeless and more understanding of why an issue occurred. With less "breathlessness" in covering stories (such as "breaking news: homeless panhandler stabs woman at gas station"), reports would not seem to suggest that the incidents with which they deal occur in a vacuum.

Thirdly, the broadcast networks especially, should be alerted to the large number of stories dealing with crimes committed by or against the homeless compared to stories dealing with the issue of homelessness.

The homeless need to realize that, as it currently operates, American journalism covers the abnormal, not the ordinary and routine aspects of American life. As a reporter commented, "We pick on everyone equally." However, the homeless may be like a lot of Americans who would like more news coverage of themselves and their organizations; they simply have to recognize that journalists only cover the most exciting, visible events in society on a given day. Unfortunately, most journalists see homelessness as a far less than exciting story. This perspective is reinforced by ratings that indicate that television news in particular draws a growing audience even when it ignores the homeless or presents them in negative ways.

Opportunities for Further Study

While my research has shown that broadcast networks present more stories dealing with crimes committed by or against the homeless than the larger social phenomenon of homelessness, it did not test for the effects of these stories on viewers. Additional study to directly measure the effects of news coverage of the homeless on ordinary Americans would be helpful and perhaps interesting. Research regarding the media's changing portrayal of the homeless would be especially helpful. In addition, there are also opportunities for additional research to test the overall audience effects generated by broadcast as opposed to print media.

With Fox News being a favorite of conservative viewers, the research opportunity exists to determine if a steady viewing diet of Fox News is negatively educating its viewers to the condition and circumstances of homelessness.

Appendix A
Statistical Analysis

This section – a statistical analysis of news stories in the broadcast and print media with content about the homeless and/or homelessness – presents the results of the analysis my assistants and I performed to determine the type of news coverage given to homeless people and the topic of homelessness by the broadcast and print media from mid-2002 through 2003.

Content Ratings by Category and Media

The statistical analysis of news content in the two news media categories examined the data categories listed below; the details for each category follow:

1. Number and percentage of stories viewed by media category (Broadcast, Print Media / Newspapers)
2. Aggregate content ratings for all reviewed news stories for each news medium (Broadcast, Print Media / Newspapers)
3. Numbers of stories viewed by Reader 1 and Reader 2 for all combined *broadcast networks* for each rating factor, and the percentage each represents of the total in the category.
4. Ratings by individual broadcast networks by reader.
5. Aggregate ratings by print/newspaper
6. Ratings by individual newspaper by reader
7. Combined comparison of Readers 1 and 2's findings for each factor by media category

Analysis Details

1. Number and percentage of stories viewed by media category: *Combined number and percentage of stories viewed by media category by both readers:*

   Broadcast – 288 story transcripts from these networks were analyzed:

   ABC News: 49 story transcripts were read, representing 17.01% of the category total.

   CBS News: 46 story transcripts were read, representing 15.97% of the category total

   CNN: 101 story transcripts were read, representing 35.07% of the category total

   FOX News: 49 story transcripts were read, representing 17.01% of the category total

   NBC News: 43 story transcripts were read, representing 14.93% of the category total

   Print – 645 stories from these papers were analyzed

   The Albuquerque Journal: 102 stories were read, representing 15.81% of the category total

   The New York Times: 367 stories were read, representing 56.90% of the category total

   The LA Times: 176 stories were read, representing 27.29% of the category total

2. Aggregate content ratings for all reviewed news stories for each news medium (Broadcast, Print Media / Newspaper): *Combined number of stories viewed/read by both readers for each rating factor, for each media category, and the percentage each represents of the total in the category.*

   Broadcast – of 288 story transcripts read:

   65 (22.6%) did not mention or deal with homelessness (0)

   87 (30.2%) mentioned the homeless/homelessness peripherally (1)

   43 (14.9%) mentioned the homeless/homelessness explicitly (2)

   93 (32.3%) reported criminal acts either by or against the homeless (3)

Print – of 645 stories read:

198 (30.70%) did not mention or deal with homelessness (0)

212 (32.9%) mentioned the homeless/homelessness peripherally (1)

195 (30.2%) mentioned the homeless/homelessness explicitly (2)

40 (6.2%) reported criminal acts either by or against the homeless (3)

3. Ratings for combined broadcast media by reader: *Numbers of stories viewed by Reader 1 and Reader 2 for all combined broadcast networks for each rating factor, and the percentage each represents of the total in the category.*

Reader 1 – of 143 story transcripts read:

35 (24.48%) did not mention or deal with homelessness (0)

39 (27.27%) mentioned the homeless/homelessness peripherally (1)

22 (15.38%) mentioned the homeless/homelessness explicitly (2)

47 (32.87%) reported criminal acts either by or against the homeless (3)

Reader 2 – of 145 story transcripts read:

30 (20.69%) did not mention or deal with homelessness (0)

48 (33.10%) mentioned the homeless/homelessness peripherally (1)

21 (14.48%) mentioned the homeless/homelessness explicitly (2)

46 (31.72%) reported criminal acts either by or against the homeless (3)

4. Ratings by individual broadcast networks by reader: *Numbers of stories viewed by Reader 1 and Reader 2 for each broadcast network for each rating factor.*

Reader 1 stories rated by network:

For ABC, of 25 story transcripts read:

6 did not mention or deal with homelessness (0)

7 mentioned the homeless/homelessness peripherally (1)

8 mentioned the homeless/homelessness explicitly (2)

4 reported criminal acts either by or against the homeless (3)
For CBS, of 22 story transcripts read:
  5 did not mention or deal with homelessness (0)
  5 mentioned the homeless/homelessness peripherally (1)
  3 mentioned the homeless/homelessness explicitly (2)
  9 reported criminal acts either by or against the homeless (3)
For CNN, of 50 story transcripts read:
  13 did not mention or deal with homelessness (0)
  20 mentioned the homeless/homelessness peripherally (1)
  3 mentioned the homeless/homelessness explicitly (2)
  14 reported criminal acts either by or against the homeless (3)
For Fox News, of 25 story transcripts read:
  7 did not mention or deal with homelessness (0)
  2 mentioned the homeless/homelessness peripherally (1)
  3 mentioned the homeless/homelessness explicitly (2)
  13 reported criminal acts either by or against the homeless (3)
For NBC, of 21 story transcripts read:
  4 did not mention or deal with homelessness (0)
  5 mentioned the homeless/homelessness peripherally (1)
  5 mentioned the homeless/homelessness explicitly (2)
  7 reported criminal acts either by or against the homeless (3)

Reader 2 stories rated by network:
For ABC, of 24 story transcripts read:
  3 did not mention or deal with homelessness (0)
  7 mentioned the homeless/homelessness peripherally (1)
  9 mentioned the homeless/homelessness explicitly (2)
  5 reported criminal acts either by or against the homeless (3)
For CBS, of 24 story transcripts read:
  6 did not mention or deal with homelessness (0)
  8 mentioned the homeless/homelessness peripherally (1)
  2 mentioned the homeless/homelessness explicitly (2)
  8 reported criminal acts either by or against the homeless (3)
For CNN, of 51 story transcripts read:
  12 did not mention or deal with homelessness (0)

21 mentioned the homeless/homelessness peripherally (1)
4 mentioned the homeless/homelessness explicitly (2)
14 reported criminal acts either by or against the homeless (3)
For Fox News, of 24 story transcripts read:
6 did not mention or deal with homelessness (0)
3 mentioned the homeless/homelessness peripherally (1)
4 mentioned the homeless/homelessness explicitly (2)
11 reported criminal acts either by or against the homeless (3)
For NBC, of 22 story transcripts read:
3 did not mention or deal with homelessness (0)
9 mentioned the homeless/homelessness peripherally (1)
2 mentioned the homeless/homelessness explicitly (2)
8 reported criminal acts either by or against the homeless (3)

5. Aggregate ratings by print/newspaper: *Numbers of stories reviewed by Reader 1 and Reader 2 for all combined newspapers for each rating factor, and the percentage each represents of the total in the category.*

Reader 1 – of 321 stories read:
125 (38.9%) did not mention or deal with homelessness (0)
79 (24.6%) mentioned the homeless/homelessness peripherally (1)
100 (31.1%) mentioned the homeless/homelessness explicitly (2)
17 (5.3%) reported criminal acts either by or against the homeless (3)

Reader 2 – of 324 stories read:
73 (22.5%) did not mention or deal with homelessness (0)
133 (41.1%) mentioned the homeless/homelessness peripherally (1)
95 (29.3%) mentioned the homeless/homelessness explicitly (2)
23 (7.1%) reported criminal acts either by or against the homeless (3)

6. Ratings by individual newspaper by reader: *Numbers of stories reviewed by Reader 1 and Reader 2 for each newspaper for each rating factor.*
    Reader 1:
    For *The Albuquerque Journal*, of 51 stories read:
    16 did not mention or deal with homelessness (0)
    15 mentioned the homeless/homelessness peripherally (1)
    16 mentioned the homeless/homelessness explicitly (2)
    4 reported criminal acts either by or against the homeless (3)
    For *The NY Times*, of 182 stories read:
    66 did not mention or deal with homelessness (0)
    52 mentioned the homeless/homelessness peripherally (1)
    56 mentioned the homeless/homelessness explicitly (2)
    8 reported criminal acts either by or against the homeless (3)
    For *The Los Angeles Times*, of 88 stories read:
    43 did not mention or deal with homelessness (0)
    12 mentioned the homeless/homelessness peripherally (1)
    28 mentioned the homeless/homelessness explicitly (2)
    5 reported criminal acts either by or against the homeless (3)

    Reader 2:
    For *The Albuquerque Journal*, of 51 stories read:
    8 did not mention or deal with homelessness (0)
    19 mentioned the homeless/homelessness peripherally (1)
    21 mentioned the homeless/homelessness explicitly (2)
    3 reported criminal acts either by or against the homeless (3)
    For *The NY Times*, of 185 stories read:
    46 did not mention or deal with homelessness (0)
    78 mentioned the homeless/homelessness peripherally (1)
    48 mentioned the homeless/homelessness explicitly (2)
    13 reported criminal acts either by or against the homeless (3)
    For *The LA Times*, of 88 stories read:
    19 did not mention or deal with homelessness (0)
    36 mentioned the homeless/homelessness peripherally (1)
    26 mentioned the homeless/homelessness explicitly (2)
    7 reported criminal acts either by or against the homeless (3)

7. Combined comparison of readers 1 and 2 findings for each factor by media category: *Side by side comparison of Reader 1's and Reader 2's results for each rating factor, for both broadcast and print news media categories.*

Table 5. Side by Side Comparison of Reader 1's and Reader 2's Results for each Rating Factor, for Broadcast News Media.

Total	Reader 1				Broadcast Media	Reader 2				Total
	0	1	2	3		0	1	2	3	
25	6	7	8	4	ABC	3	7	9	5	24
22	5	5	3	9	CBS	6	8	2	8	24
50	13	20	3	14	CNN	12	21	4	14	51
25	7	2	3	13	Fox	6	3	4	11	24
21	4	5	5	7	NBC	3	9	2	8	22
143	35	39	22	47	288	30	48	21	46	145
49.7%	24.5%	27.3%	15.4%	32.9%		20.7%	33.1%	14.5%	31.7%	50.3%

Table 6. Side-by-Side Comparison of Reader 1's and Reader 2's Results for Each Rating Factor, for Print News Media.

Total	Reader 1				Print Media	Reader 2				Total
	0	1	2	3		0	1	2	3	
51	16	15	16	4	Alb Jrnl	8	19	21	3	51
182	66	52	56	8	NY Times	46	78	48	13	185
88	43	12	28	5	LA Times	19	36	26	7	88
321	125	79	100	17	645	73	133	95	23	324
49.8%	38.9%	24.6%	31.2%	5.3%		22.5%	41.0%	29.5%	7.1%	50.2%

Appendix B
Questions Asked of the Homeless

Although in this research you will only be identified by a number, please give your name and where you live. (Street, shelter etc).

What do you think of the media's coverage of the homeless both locally and nationally?

Has your perception of the way the media cover the homeless changed since you became homeless?

Depending on answer to 3), if the response is negative, ask:

    3(a) what do you think would be a healthy way for the media to cover the homeless?

Where do you believe the average person in Albuquerque gets most of his or her knowledge about the homeless?

How do you think the typical reporter gets most of his or her knowledge about the homeless?

Do you have anything else you would like to say about the way the media cover the homeless?

Let's suppose you were invited to a meeting of media heads here in Albuquerque and they asked you how you think the media could improve their coverage of the homeless. What would you say?

Appendix C
Interviews with the Homeless

The following interviews with the homeless at Joy Junction were conducted by my research assistant and first reader.

Respondent Number One

The interviewer asked Joy Junction Respondent Number One what she thought of the media's coverage of the homeless both locally and nationally.

She responded, "I don't … watch TV hardly, as far as newspapers, I haven't seen anything."

The interviewer asked, "Okay, radio? Anything?"

"No, I don't listen," this person responded.

The interviewer then asked if her perception of the way the media covers the homeless had changed since she became homeless. She said that it had and "in a way, it's helped me … and it helps me see what they go through, as well."

However, the respondent said she did not know what would be a good way for the media to cover the homeless. She told the interviewer that she thought the average person in Albuquerque gets most of his or her information about the homeless by talking to other people and that the reporter learns most of his or her knowledge about the homeless by "asking questions and getting answers."

At that point, the interviewer asked just of whom reporters were asking questions. "The homeless," the respondent replied. "If they ask the homeless, they'll get, you know.

She told the interviewer that if she were invited to a meeting of media executives and asked how the media could improve their coverage of the homeless, she would tell them they need to "send more people out to interview the homeless, see how they live and what makes them survive, and how they get around, different ways that people, categories, because everybody has their own little issues, and that would cover most of them."

Respondent Number Two

Respondent Number Two at Joy Junction told the interviewer that he thought the media's coverage of the homeless both locally and nationally was "terrible. (There's) no coverage. All they want to do is show the negative side and none of the positive."

Asked if he thought that applied both nationally and locally, the respondent said, "Everywhere. No matter where I've been, it's always been the crime involved, never the plight of the homeless, per se, to the homeless. You don't ever hear their side of it; you always hear the negative side."

However, when asked if his perception of the way the media cover the homeless had changed since he became homeless, Respondent Number Two had a surprising response.

"No, I've never been homeless," he said. "I'm here under God's instruction." He said he had no idea about a "healthy way" for the media to cover the homeless. "I have no instruction for them," he said.

Number Two said he thinks the average person gets most of his or her information about the homeless from the media. "Mostly it's all negative," he said. "Very few times except here at Joy Junction has there been anything done in a positive manner."

He thinks the typical reporter gets his or her information about the homeless in the same way, "Media events and by police reports and things like that they get off the street," he said. "Just everything I see on TV or read in the newspaper or hear on the radio is all negative attitude. They need to come and find out what they're talking about before they ever print anything. Period."

Respondent Number Three

Respondent Number Three said that, in her opinion, the media in California show the homeless in a very bad light. She continued. "Here, we're really not getting that much for the simple reason, homeless people need a lot of things other than food, shelter and clothing. We need medical, we need just basic simple things. We also want respect. We don't want you to judge us because we're homeless; we want you to judge us by our attitude and our actions at times. The media judges us in a way that we're all homeless people are bums, we're drunks, we're druggies, and there are some of us that are (alcoholics) and druggies, and there are a good majority of us that are, like my husband and myself, who are NOT in that way. We don't steal, do drugs, we don't drink alcohol. A lot of us just smoke cigarettes and drink soda pop and water, and that's about it."

However, she said that nationally the homeless are shown in a negative light. She then described how her perception of how the media cover the homeless has changed since she became homeless. "It's gotten worse than better. We're being beat upon, stomped," she said.

With that in mind, the interviewer asked the respondent what would be a better way for the media to cover the homeless?

Respondent Number Three responded quickly, suggesting that the media should portray the homeless "how we look, how we act. As in the Bible, treat others as you would want to be treated. Other than that, you're missing out on some good friendly people who are homeless."

Asked how the average person in Albuquerque gets most of their knowledge about the homeless, she said (not answering the question), "They snub their nose at us. People lack respect as an every day person, even though a lot of us don't have jobs, as normal human being."

Number Three said reporters learn about the homeless by what she dubbed "second hand information," saying "Like if somebody in their own family goes to a store and sees a homeless person sitting next to a grocery store asking for change just for a bottle of beer or a ... a lot of us just want to survive. We want food, we want shelter; we want clothing. All we ask. Not like 'give me some change so I can get a bottle of beer.' I've seen it happening, like back in California when we were in Bakersfield. But there are those of us who are honest and just want food. For an example, my husband and I were in Bakersfield. I had to panhandle just so we'd have our cigarettes, our soda and our food. And everyday a lot of time, it was Arby's. That's all we had for survival ... My husband has been sober for close to 30-some odd years now ... He's also lost a lot of weight since his two heart attacks almost four years ago, for a man his age."

In a rambling answer, she said she would like to see the homeless be treated with more respect. "Donations of any kind helps. It's not like we're going to be going out into the streets and mugging you. A lot of us are not like that," she said. "There's a guy out in Marin County, California. He has a radio talk show. He lumps all of us homeless people as bums. We're not. We're average people with an average everyday life. We just require food, clothing and shelter and ... this bum did this, this bum did that. We're not that way. Up in Seattle you see so many people sleeping in front of businesses at night, because the shelters are inadequate, it's especially worse up there than it is here ... places to go for a hot shower, nice warm clothing, places to go for understanding ... We're not going to hurt you. None of us want to hurt people."

Asked what she would tell media executives about how they could improve their coverage of the homeless, this respondent said "Help us out with the job if there's one available."

When the interviewer repeated the question, Respondent Number Three said, "Give us work. Give us a chance. Don't judge us by how we look. Just because we dress in old ratty jeans and a t-shirt and coats don't mean we're bad people."

Respondent Number Four

Respondent Number Four was unsure about the way the media cover the homeless nationally, though he did say "you see stuff on the news all the time."

"Locally I don't see to see enough stuff about Joy Junction," he said "and locally Joy Junction, in my opinion, is probably doing the best job around this area, but I don't see that much about it on the TV that I watch. But of course we don't get cable."

This respondent said his perception of the way the media covers the homeless had changed since he became homeless. "I think there's probably more influence on what can be done to help the homeless," he said, "and that there is a homeless plight that's probably not being addressed to its fullest extent. You didn't use to hear anything about the homeless but them being in alleys and stuff. Now you hear about people trying to help the homeless, and that's ... better than what it used to be."

"The average person in Albuquerque," Respondent Number Four said, "gets much of his or her information about the homeless by a word of mouth exchange."

However, he was unsure about where reporters turn to get their information. "That I'm not sure I can answer properly," he said. "Maybe people on the street; maybe somebody from a shelter calls them and tells them something. They don't seem to be researching it that much, there's not that many in-depth news clips about it on TV. I'm not sure how they get it, to tell you the truth."

This respondent had some words of advice for those concerned about the plight of the homeless. "They ought to be coming out and researching it," he said. "Go shelter by shelter and see what people have to offer to the homeless people, and how they can help them. They ought to at least look into the people are doing help for the homeless and find out why they're doing it and what they can offer."

Asked to give advice to media executives about improving their coverage of the homeless, Respondent Number Four said he would, "tell them to go out and look at the shelters personally, take a look at what they're doing for the people, and how the average citizen can help those shelters help those other people."

Respondent Number Five

Asked what he thought of the media's coverage of the homeless, Respondent Number Five said he would not describe it as being negative, but more of "a cry for help." He said, "There are definitely (bad and good) ... in every group ... If they do show a lot of homeless people, some of them are not trying to help themselves. They're in the system, so people need to be educated to know that there are people that want to get back into society, so to speak. And I think they should show that type of person more. Locally or nationally."

This respondent said that although his perception of the way the media cover the homeless has not changed since he became homeless, he has become "more educated ... This is the first time I've been experiencing this."

Respondent Number Six

Asked what she thought about the media's coverage of the homeless, Respondent Number Six said "I see Jeremy (Reynalds) on the TV sometimes, when he's asking for donations or help with money or blankets."

When asked if her perception of the way the media cover the homeless had changed since she became homeless, this respondent laughed and said "In a way. It hasn't really changed." She added, though, that she had a positive perception of media coverage of the homeless.

When asked where she thought the average person in Albuquerque gets most of his or her information about media coverage of the homeless, Respondent Number Six said "From the rescue mission, a bunch of them don't have a place to watch TV, so they can't get it from the media."

This respondent said she thought a typical reporter relies on "Being out there in the streets, being homeless," to get his or her knowledge about the homeless.

Regarding what she would tell media executive about how they could improve their coverage of the homeless, this respondent laughed and said she would tell them they need to improve.

Respondent Number Seven

Respondent Number Seven praised local media coverage of the homeless, saying, "Locally I would say it's one of the best that I've seen because I've seen 'em on TV. For me, being a homeless person, I appreciate everything that they do here for me. Nationally, I have never seen it. If it's like it is now, it should be wonderful."

This respondent said his perception of media coverage of the homeless had not changed since he became homeless.

The average person learns about the homeless, he said, "off the streets and the people that's been here before. Like myself, I've been asked quite a few times, where is there a good shelter. And I've told them where it is."

Number Seven said he did not know where reporters looked for information concerning the homeless.

When asked how the media could more effectively cover the homeless, he said that he would like to see them do more stories and be more aware of what goes on at Joy Junction. "I've done a lot of work out here, done a lot of stuff, for me, it's been good. I've got a lot of stuff that I never knew before, which Mr. Reynalds (has) helped me with. Like Bible study and going back to church and stuff like that. It's been great for me. But sometimes, when you forget the Lord, it gets to you."

Respondent Number Eight

Respondent Number Eight stated the media should give more coverage to the homeless. "I don't think there's enough coverage on it, locally or nationally," he said. "They should probably have a little bit more and talk to the people and see where they're coming from."

This respondent said his perception of the way the media cover the homeless has changed since he became homeless. "Cause now that I'm there, I see where they're coming from," he said, "and I don't think it's a very bad thing, especially living at Joy Junction. They help you out, help you get back on your feet."

Respondent Number Eight said a healthy way for the media to cover the homeless would be to talk to a variety of different people "and see what their thoughts are and where they're coming from; see how they can help them."

"The average person in Albuquerque," this respondent said, "gets most of his information about the homeless by seeing people on the streets. But that probably doesn't help too much if (they are not homeless) themselves. Agencies for the homeless help in providing reporters with information," he said. Just by places like this, getting calls and filming from here, and seeing how the people live," he said.

When offered the opportunity to tell the media how they could improve their coverage of the homeless, Number Eight said he would advise them to "talk to the homeless, and see where they're coming from, so they know how they live. A lot of people who aren't homeless don't know how things are out there, especially for people who don't have a place like Joy Junction to stay at. Those ones are worse off than we are here."

Respondent Number Nine

Respondent Number Nine said he had not seen any media coverage of the homeless, and that his perception of the way the media cover the homeless had changed since he became homeless. "Yeah, I've seen 'em here," he said.

When asked how he thought the average person gets information about the homeless, this respondent number initially said "I don't understand what you're wanting. What the average person thinks of the homeless?"

When the question was repeated, he responded, "I personally think that a lot of them think that just because you're homeless, you're scum on the earth."

When asked how people come to that conclusion, Number Nine said, "Some of the homeless, they have caused a bad reputation because they steal and what have you."

This respondent said he thinks reporters learn about the homeless from other people and "people that contact the media and stuff."

Asked what advice he could give media executives about improving their coverage of the homeless, Respondent Number Nine said, "they need to maybe interview a little more, get some of the personal stories of the people, why they're homeless and things like that."

Respondent Number 10

Regarding what he thought about the media's coverage of the homeless, Respondent Number Ten said, "The coverage in Albuquerque is very good, but there needs to be more national attention paid to the issue."

Asked to clarify what he meant by saying the coverage in Albuquerque is "very good," this respondent said, "In comparison to other cities I've lived in, I see commercials and coverage here locally, versus in other cities I see none. So by very good, I mean saturating the market."

Respondent Number Ten confirmed that his perception of the way the media cover the homeless has changed for the worse. "They're not portraying a true picture," he complained. "I think. I'm basing that on what I experienced in other cities. Here it seems to be pretty realistic, but in Las Vegas, Nevada, where I came from, it was definitely painting a picture that wasn't realistic. Not showing the true magnitude of the problem or the needs of the people."

This respondent thinks that a healthier way for the media to cover the homeless would be to talk directly to homeless people. "It seems like you just see staff or administrators talking, versus some of the people," he said. "Perhaps getting people fresh off their street as they're coming in, find out how they came to the circumstances that they came to be here. Things like that."

Respondent Number Ten initially indicated that he thought the average person gets most of his or her information about the homeless by word of mouth from other people. From the "police department also. I wouldn't say it would be the media, because a lot of homeless people don't watch TV, you know?"

When reminded by the interviewer that he was being asked about the average person, Respondent Number Ten said, "That would be from the news. Either that or directly coming in here with donations. That would also be a good time to maybe fill them in more upon the needs and missions and goals."

"Reporters," he said, "probably get their information by relying on other people who do research for them. I wouldn't say it would be done hands-on, I think they're kind of out of touch when they come out to talk to the people. I would think probably be done internally with the news agency ... That's how it's done, I'm assuming, with any story they have to research and find out certain things and that's passed on to the reporter, and it's read from the script, rather than actually on-the-spot."

Respondent Number Ten said that the media need to find a newer and more positive way to cover the homeless. "I think they need to perhaps break away from the stereotype of the cliché of the dirty ... unshaved type, you know what I mean. That's been a common thing and nowadays, people from all walks of life, in financial areas, find themselves homeless. It's no longer just people that are lazy or don't want to work, it affects everyone now and it seems to be a real problem."

Asked what he would say to media heads if given the opportunity to tell them how they could improve their coverage of the homeless, this respondent said that he would encourage them to talk directly to the homeless and find out the situations they encountered that resulted in their becoming homeless.

Asked how that would improve coverage, Number Ten said, "I think it would give more of a realistic tone to the story that people can relate to. Everyone's been in tough times and situations. Perhaps by relating their story, people could relate to that."

Respondent Number 11

Respondent Number Eleven said she thinks that media coverage of the homeless, "stinks," both locally and nationally, adding, "Because they just portray all homeless people as dirty, filthy, scroungy people out there just begging for money, or don't want to work or worthless, and they don't want to portray what a homeless person is. Especially Channel 13 in Albuquerque. They've done several pieces on homeless people and they always get the homeless that are filthy and been on the street corner with signs begging for money with their hair all matted. That's not me."

This respondent said that she has been homeless for five years and her perception of the way the media cover the homeless has not changed in that time. "No, I've always thought they did a rotten job about it. They don't really portray the real homeless. Not all homeless people are like that. Some of us are clean and trying to make a good life for ourselves and have made the choices to make changes. I'm trying to make them changes and they don't care. They want people to think we're all trash."

Asked why she thought that, Respondent Number Eleven was unsure. "I've always said there is never a three-minute news show that shows anything positive. They show the worst in everything."

This respondent said that media should visit Joy Junction and other shelters and interview some of the homeless guests. "These are people who are really trying to make sure they're not homeless anymore. Come out here and talk to the ones who need help and want help and are trying to help themselves. So maybe people would understand sometimes there's just unfortunate situations that make people homeless and maybe if we could just give this person a little edge, they'd be alright. And they'd be better and they could have a normal life."

This respondent had firm convictions about how she believed the average person in Albuquerque learned about the homeless.

"From the people they see standing on the street corner begging. The filthy, dirty, nasty ones, or the … homeless man that robbed someone for a few dollars and killed them. They don't see the poor little homeless girl working in the laundry room so she can have a place to stay and better her life. They don't. I bet you could ask 90% of people in Albuquerque about Joy Junction and some of them have never heard of it. Never heard of it. My aunt never heard of this place until I started staying here."

Asked how the typical reporter gets most of his or her knowledge about the homeless, Respondent Number Eleven said she thinks they are "stupid" when it comes to dealing with the homeless. "They portray them as bums out there on the street who want to be homeless because they want to spend their Social Security check on dope and drinking all the time, that's what they think a homeless person is," this respondent replied. "They don't realize that a homeless person is out here trying to get a step ahead in life, trying to better them self. They don't realize that a homeless person can be pregnant and out here trying to do good and stay off dope. But they'll glorify the ones that stay out there smoking the dope, and that's why they're homeless."

She also she that did not think the media would do positive stories on homeless people who were trying to better themselves. "They won't help us. But they'll get on TV and preach about the poor man on the street corner who chooses to drink his social security check up when he could have a place," Respondent Number Eleven said. "They'll glorify him and help him get a place and in two months he's homeless again because he can't pay his rent because he's drinking all the money up," she said. "But they won't come out here and help someone with kids who just need a little help. They can't afford to pay first month's rent and last month's rent and deposit all at the same time. Or me, I'm pregnant. I can't afford to pay all that. But I'm willing to try ..."

This respondent complained further about media coverage of the homeless. "They put 'em all (the homeless) on TV and people call 'em with cash donations to help. My mom and dad even done it. They put homeless people on TV and if they just had a little help, they could be OK. But they don't tell you that two months later, they're not in their apartment anymore because they smoked that money up on crack. But they don't come out here to people that really need that. They'll pull someone off the interstate underpass and help them." She elaborated further. "I wish they (the media) would come out here and do some of the little pieces they do for the people off the streets on some of us, and try and help us, the people that really want and need the help. The people that just can't quite get ahead in life because it's too hard, but they want to. I wish they would come out here and show a homeless person that's struggling to do good, to do things right, instead of a homeless person that's gonna go drink their life away, or smoke their life away. I think it's ridiculous how they do things in Albuquerque and nationwide."

"The situation is the same nationwide," she continued, explaining that she has lived all over America. "They'll help the ones that'll smoke up a crack pipe or drink up a 40 on a daily basis, but they won't go help the ones in the homeless shelters that are really trying to get ahead. I wish some of the news channels would actually come out here and see the ones that want help, and want a life."

Asked what she would tell media heads about how they could improve coverage of the homeless, Respondent Number Eleven said, "Leave the drunks and the druggies out of it. They want to be homeless. Help the ones that are trying to help their self, the ones that got a job and they just don't have enough to get anyplace. Or the ones that are off drugs and going through rehab and recovery."

Shifting to the form of coverage that could really help, this respondent said, "Because people would understand that there's really people out there that are homeless that aren't homeless because they're on drugs and alcohol; they're just needing a little boost in life."

Explaining her situation, Number Eleven said she was not staying at Joy Junction because she chose to. "I'm here because of a lot of unfortunate things that's happened in my life. And I made choices to change them, and I'm changing it. I think the media should help get coverage to the people are trying to change their lives and show Albuquerque and America what a homeless person on the right track in life is doing and looks like, instead of a homeless person on a downward spiral. Because that's all America sees, is the homeless person on a downward spiral. They see the homeless person that froze to death underneath a bridge, but they don't hear the story behind it, he was passed out and couldn't call the homeless shelter that would have let him sleep there."

She continued, "The news don't tell you that, that he was drunk, his alcohol level was four times the legal limit, or he was so coked out or cracked out. None of 'em tell you that; they make you feel sorry for the people who don't care about themselves. There's people that are homeless that care about themselves. And I think they ought to show America more of those people, instead of the people who don't care about their selves."

Respondent Number 12

Respondent Number Twelve said that she feels media coverage of the homeless is too limited. "They cover us, but they only cover us during holiday times. Any other time, the coverage is covered negatively," (both locally and nationally) she said.

This respondent said that her perception of the way the media cover the homeless has not really changed since she became homeless. "I would have to say that before I became homeless, I never really paid attention," she said. "Now that I am homeless, the only time I think the media covers the homeless in a positive manner is during the holidays, and any other time would be negatively."

She continued, "A more healthy way for the media to cover the homeless would be for them not to think that all of the homeless are bad people. Not all homeless are drug addicts and thieves. The homeless are homeless for a reason, 'cause we didn't pay our bills, or domestic violence, or whatever it may be. But the media should take more of a compassionate look into the homeless situation."

According to Respondent Number Twelve, the average person in Albuquerque gets most of his or her knowledge about the homeless through a family member or maybe someone close to them becoming homeless. "If it's a church or person of the clergy, maybe it's through their congregation," she said. "A lot of your rich people – and I hate to classify anybody – but a lot of your rich people are scared to death of homeless people and they don't want anything to do with us, you know, or anybody homeless, whether it's becoming a volunteer here at Joy Junction or anywhere. They stay away from us."

The interviewer then asked this respondent, "Let me clarify about if it's clergy or if it's the church. What do you mean by that, that's how they get their information?"

"Calvary, for instance," Respondent Number Twelve answered, "they work with us one-on-one and to them, we're not a number; we're a name; we're a person. Which whether you're homeless or not, you are a person. I came to be homeless through situations beyond my control, and I chose to remain homeless so that I can strengthen my walk with God, and through Calvary (Chapel) and through Joy Junction, I've noticed that Calvary takes more of a hands-on approach with Joy Junction and with the homeless."

Respondent Number Twelve was unable to answer how the typical reporter gets most of his or her information about the homeless.

This respondent thought the media need to be more compassionate when dealing with and portraying the homeless. "They need to (tell) the public through the media that not all homeless people are bad people, not all homeless people are alcoholics or drug addicts or whatever," she said. "Everybody has a different story for being here. It needs to go through the media to know that if it wasn't for Joy Junction and the Good Shepherd and the Salvation Army and different places like that, they would be telling stories more about people dead because of hypothermia, than anything. I think they need to take a more compassionate look at the homeless ... That means the media has to show us more compassion so that the public will look at us that way.

Asked what she would tell media executives if invited to help them improve their coverage of the homeless, Respondent Number Twelve answered that she would ask them to cover the homeless year round, not just at the holiday seasons. "We're not just homeless during November and December; we're homeless through the year. They need to give us the same coverage they give us during November and December to where the public will return the donations, because you know, Joy Junction lives on donations and without that, we don't eat," this respondent said. "We aren't clothed, we don't have roofs over our head, the light and utilities don't get paid, so the media needs to take the same approach to the homeless year round that they take two months of the year. They should be year round instead of just November and December.

Respondent Number 13

According to Respondent Number Thirteen, media coverage of the homeless can sometimes be "pretty harsh. "Remember not very long ago there was a woman shot at and he (the shooter) wasn't even homeless. He was a drug addict and they blamed it on the homeless. Sometimes we are stereotyped," this respondent said. "They put down the homeless even though they've been homeless themselves, and now that they're not, they think they're better." However, in an apparently contradictory statement, Number Thirteen continued by saying "And the media, I can't really say because I haven't really heard them talk about the homeless, because for the past couple of months since I became homeless, I don't watch TV that much ... But sometimes when I go places and stuff and they think we're homeless, it's like, you gotta get out of here, you can't sit here in the lobby because you look homeless because you have a back pack or something with you. That I think is very offensive."

This respondent suggested that a better way for the media to treat the homeless would be with "more respect. "They could become homeless themselves and how would they like to be treated like a nobody, because everybody could be a nobody sometime," she said. "I do believe that a lot of us are criticized and put down as though we're peasants, because ... they don't really want to have nothing to do with us. I had a home, I have children,

I have grandchildren. And for them to be treating a lot of people the way they do because we're homeless now is very degrading to me."

Asked whether her perception of how the media cover the homeless had changed since she became homeless, this respondent said that it has. "Definitely, because of the way I'm treated because I'm homeless."

Respondent Number Thirteen said that the average person in Albuquerque probably learns about the homeless "from people that don't even know what it's like to be homeless. Probably just off the street from somebody that had a bad result from somebody that's homeless."

Asked how reporters learn about the homeless, Number Thirteen said, "Maybe just from anybody. It doesn't even have to be from somebody that's homeless; it could just be any Joe from off the street. And this person doesn't even know anything, but if they asked me, I would tell them about things that are going on in my life in the past two months since I became homeless."

Asked what she would tell a group of media executives if invited to help them improve their coverage of the homeless, Respondent Number Thirteen said, "I would say, come here and join the club and find out what it's like before you criticize or anything. It isn't like a good feeling to become homeless and not know where you're gonna go ..."

Respondent Number 14

Asked what he thought about the media's coverage of the homeless, Respondent Number Fourteen said he was "extremely offended" by it. He elaborated, saying, "The majority of the time they are not showing anybody doing anything productive about it. All I've seen are, they show scenes of homeless people and they start talking about crime rate, drug rates, and particularly here locally that's getting worse in the last month or so ... Particularly the downtown area."

He continued, "Nationally I see that on several of the news [shows], when they start focusing on the major cities, they'll focus on somebody that's homeless, a bag lady, somebody that's pushing a shopping cart, and they'll say 'We have a high increase in crime.'"

Asked whether his perception of the way the media cover the homeless had changed since he became homeless, this respondent said that it had.

"Before that, even though I tried helping as much as I could whenever I met somebody homeless, my perception was sort of, they needed to make an effort to get out of there. It was their fault," he said. "Since then, I've learned it's not their fault at all times. It's circumstances beyond their control a lot of times."

Respondent Number Fourteen said that it would be a very positive thing for the media to start talking to some of the people who are homeless. "Get their stories, find out exactly what's happening," he said. "Now a lot of them out there right now shouldn't be out on the streets because frankly they have mental problems severe enough where they should be in some sort of a controlled environment where they won't hurt themselves and where they won't suffer because they don't realize what's going on around them."

He added, "We've had several come in here in the middle of the night under police escort because they're found laying in ditches and sewers and not because they're drunk or drugged, but because they just lay down and didn't realize where they were. I'm not saying that there isn't a problem with booze or drugs out there, but that's not the whole reason."

This respondent said that television news provides the average Albuquerque resident with most of the information he knows about the homeless. "A little bit from the newspapers," he said, "but that's extremely rare at times, and it's rare that it's anything beneficial or good relating to the homeless people. Every time it's negative." Respondent Number Fourteen had definite feelings about some media personnel whom he had seen while staying at Joy Junction. "I've noticed several here from the TV crews and they're usually standing around against the wall with their arms folded, almost their lips curled, snarling at people. The so-called stars on the evening news," he said, "the majority of them will go to a story and they obviously look bored when they're out here trying to cover it. The only time I've seen any real interest was that time with that Cuban couple, and everybody gave them a lot of attention, and that created a lot of negative feelings with the other residents, because they thought they were being neglected at the expense of these other two people."

"I've never encountered in the last year or so TV, radio, papers, anybody asking anything to benefit the homeless," he continued, "unless they were responding to the of the so-called 'pitches' for donations. But other than talking about donations that were needed at certain times of year, all they focus on is the negative effects."

If asked by the media how to improve coverage of the homeless, Respondent Number Fourteen said he would tell them to "abandon the 'attitude' and try to talk to the people as people. Find out their stories." He added, "A lot of them are there because of unfortunate circumstances. Some of them are there because of drugs and alcohol, some of them because they don't have the mental faculties to take care of themselves, but you're not going to find out unless you talk to them. And don't come in there with the bright cameras, because all that does is scare people away. Basically they need to try to get in there in a subdued atmosphere one-on-one, maybe offer some coffee and sandwiches to somebody, and talk to 'em on a human level."

Respondent Number 15

Respondent Number Fifteen said that he doesn't think there is very much coverage of the homeless by the homeless and what there is isn't very good.

His perception of the way the media cover the homeless has changed since he became homeless. "Well, yeah, didn't want to hear about it when you weren't homeless," he said, "but now you are, you do want to hear about it and see how the other people are getting along, or what they're doing in other places to help them."

The respondent said he thinks members of the media should walk with the homeless for a week. "See what they gotta do," he said. "Go to St. Martin's or HCH (Health Care for the Homeless), or wherever they gotta go. Stay on the streets for five hours before their next meal, or just walk with 'em to just see what they gotta do. Walk a mile in their shoes, so to speak."

Asked how he believes the average person gets most of his or her knowledge about the homeless, the respondent said that they do so at Christmas time during the holidays. "That's the only time you see anything about it," he said, "unless there's somebody unfortunate enough to die in the cold, and that's the only time you hear about 'em."

According to Respondent Number Fifteen, even when the media do cover the homeless, they really don't. "They just tell you there's a need here or a need there, they show you the chow lines, and that's it. I don't think they have a clue, I really don't think they have a clue. They come in here, they set up their stuff, they ask some questions and they bail. They go home to their families, they go home to their house, what do they care? It's just another story. Not really, anyway. They just need to do a better job. They need to *do* a job." He added, "If it wasn't during the holidays, if you were to ask a reporter where the homeless are today, they couldn't tell you. They'd tell you downtown Albuquerque. They wouldn't know how to tell you where to look. They wouldn't know anything about where they're at or anything. They couldn't tell you anything. They don't know anything about the homeless."

Respondent Number 16

Respondent Number Sixteen said she thought that, while the media's coverage of the homeless was "okay," they could still probably "do a little bit better. I think they stereotype sometimes, so that's the problem I have, but I haven't seen very much lately."

The respondent said, "Nationally, I would say they stereotype. I haven't seen too much locally on the homeless. Some people, since I've been staying here, a couple of friends I have in the area, they're like, 'Oh yeah.' I was watching the news and we were on the news, this place was being covered, and they didn't say anything bad about it, I guess it was interesting."

Her perception of the way the media cover the homeless hasn't changed since she became homeless, Respondent Number Sixteen said. "A healthier way for the national media to cover the homeless," she said, would be to "try to make it a little bit more personal, or try to get more information before they put everybody in one little thing." She added, "Maybe they just need to combine their stories a little bit better, all the reporters, instead of just skimming over some things and leaving details out ... They act like their opinions are fact, and just kind of changing things, are the problems I have, what I've seen in other places, that they've done."

This respondent thought that average people in Albuquerque get their knowledge about the homeless "from the broadcast news both local and national and maybe the newspaper," adding, "Other than maybe just what they see if they're downtown. I don't really know."

Asked by the interviewer what she meant by her last statement, Number Sixteen commented, "I know that some cities have a bigger homeless problem, you know some bigger cities. You'll see a whole bunch of people in parks, or in cities that have really big tall buildings, like in alleyways; you'll see people lined up along the buildings. Sometimes it can be right around the corner from the shopping district, or something. I haven't seen too much of that here, but I'm sure there is some of it, so maybe downtown (average) people might see at night, people that looked a little, the average person might feel a little threatened by, because maybe they're dirty, or sleeping on something by a building."

The respondent said that reporters might typically get their information about the homeless by "probably just by going to a location where they might be, we might be, and maybe like wondering around, they'll talk to some people there, or maybe they'll just go and talk to the people that run the place. They might interview a couple of people. I think the average person or average reporter wouldn't want to spend too much time there, unless it was something major." "That's because," she added, "they were probably just trying to get the story together as fast as they could, that's my opinion, it might make them a little leery, just get out of there as fast we can and get it over with."

Number Sixteen said that if she were asked by media executives how they could improve coverage of the homeless, she would tell them to quit putting all the homeless in one category and looking down on them. "They have to change their attitude a little bit," she said. "They also need to try to interview more, actually, instead of having one or two people say something on camera, people that make it. Maybe have a group of people talking about whatever the topic's gonna be, instead of just listening to the reporter the whole time. Just like get more people's opinions that are actually there."

Respondent Number 17

Respondent Number Seventeen said that he thinks the media's coverage of the homeless is more positive than negative compared to other cities. "A lot of places, it's lots more negative as far as having people on your streets," he said. "Places like New York, you have this thing where police don't allow you to sleep on the benches and how it disrupts the city."

This respondent, who said his perception of media coverage of the homeless had not changed since he became homeless, suggested a few healthier ways for the media to cover the homeless. "Instead of putting them down as derelicts and people who have ruined the neighborhood," he said, "cover stories like why people are homeless and how they got that way, then people can understand it can happen to anybody."

Respondent Number Seventeen said he thought most people in Albuquerque get their knowledge about the homeless from the news. "Or you got those people who automatically assume (when they see) a couple of guys standing by the side of the road with signs saying 'Will work for food' and they think it's the whole homeless population doing that."

The respondent said that he thinks the average reporter gets his knowledge about the homeless from a number of different sources such as shelters and neighborhoods. According to him, reporters routinely consider the homeless to be alcoholics or drug addicts, "instead of … people (who) just happen to have a bad turn in life, got laid off their job and there's no more jobs in town. There's places where those jobs close down and they don't get those next two paychecks and the next thing you know, they're out on the street."

If asked to advise media executives how they could improve their coverage of the homeless, Respondent Number Seventeen said he would tell them to ask the homeless themselves for their stories – not someone else. "Second hand information is the worst kind … of information," he said. "It's families, doctors, lawyers, Indian chiefs, all become homeless. Go up to that individual and … maybe more people will be willing to help out."

Respondent Number 18

Respondent Number 18 said she doesn't think the media provide much coverage of the "plight" of the homeless.

Asked what she meant by the word "plight," this respondent said, "Well, it is a problem. Some of the facilities are good; there are a lot of facilities in Albuquerque. I've (been to) places like Waco, Texas, where there's absolutely nothing for homeless people, so these facilities are good. But people are homeless for different reasons; some people through no fault of their own lost their houses (and) their jobs. Some of them are alcoholics, some are drug addicts; some of them have just given up. Some of them don't like rules and regulations, so there are a lot of different reasons."

Continuing, she said that while these reasons for becoming homeless are not adequately dealt with on media coverage of the homeless, "you can't help everybody across the board, you can't say, 'Oh, I'll help the drug addict the same way I'll help the alcoholic' or 'I'll help the homeless who lost their jobs' the same way I'll help the drug addict. It should be more individualized. I've hardly ever seen anything on TV about the homeless people, other than the panhandling downtown that has gotten aggressive. That's the only thing I've seen since I've been here."

Concerning national coverage, this respondent said she had not seen much.

When asked whether the national coverage she had seen had been negative or positive, Respondent Number 18 identified herself as being from the New York / New Jersey area. "When Ed Koch was mayor," she said, "he started this campaign to get the homeless off the streets. He figured if you can rehabilitate them; that would be a positive step in the right direction. He took this one woman who used to park herself in front of this guy's restaurant and took her off the streets, gave her a job, sort of rehabilitated her, and within a month or so, she was right back where she was. Sometimes the ideas work, and some people just can't handle the pressure of living in society, so they take to the streets because there are no rules and regulations."

Respondent Number 18 said her perception of the way the media cover the homeless had not changed since she had been homeless.

Asked what she thought would be a more healthy way for the media to cover the homeless, this respondent said that, in her opinion, the coverage needs to be more "individualized," that there are a variety of reasons why people end up being homeless, and all those contributing factors should not be lumped into one aggregate under the homeless banner. "Like I say, you can't lump each situation all into one thing and say, 'Oh, we're homeless, let's do this or that' because it won't apply to everyone."

Respondent Number 18 commented about the problems she perceived at domestic violence shelters. "The woman that's been battered, there's no strength left to her except to get to that shelter to be safe," she said. "But I've seen a lot of times where they don't actually help that woman, they'll say, and I've heard this for a fact, 'Okay, you can sleep here for 24 hours, but then you have to get out and go do this, and go do that.' I mean, why not just help her … it wasn't her fault that she had to leave her home. She had to give up everything to go to that shelter, where the perpetrator gets to live wherever he wants, but she's now got the status of being homeless."

Respondent Number 18 continued. "Why not open up facilities where she can get on her feet and help her find a job if need be. And then do periodic checkups once you get her established. I know because I've been in that situation. You can't do it on your own. And I've worked really hard at this point to get out of that situation and it just goes in a circle. If you get results in one area, you won't in another. And I think if I was out looking for a job on my own – 'cause I've not been homeless all my life, it's just been within the last year or so – I would not have … all these programs. I would not have to go through all this other stuff, red tape and all, I would go find a job, find an apartment, food, clothing, and shelter. Why all these programs that aren't necessary? Again, it's not individualized. Each thing should be for whatever specific need they have. So it's really, really tough."

Reminded by the interviewer that the question was what would be a more healthy way for the media to cover the homeless, the respondent reiterated that the coverage needed to be individualized.

"Like I said," the respondent replied again, "each situation is different and you can't just (say) 'oh, the homeless, they need help.' Yes they need help, but how?"

Responding to the question about how the average person in Albuquerque gets most of his or her knowledge about the homeless, Number 18 said (laughing), "Probably going through Concrete Park downtown" (laughs again). "That's where they're all hanging out, or you can go at noon and see them standing in line, and panhandling."

The respondent said she was unaware where the average reporter got most of his or her information from about the homeless. "Unless a newspaper decides to take an interest and send somebody out to do a report," she said. "How do they do it? Do they go where they see the most homeless? Do they go to shelters? I really don't know."

Asked how she would advise media executives interesting in improving their reporting on the homeless, Number 18 said "Is there such a thing as unbiased reporting anymore?" She added, "Best thing I could say is, you have to actually feel it. You have to actually feel what you're talking about when you do talk to people about it that are in trouble … people say unless you've actually experienced it, you don't know."

Respondent Number 19

Asked what he thought of the media's coverage of the homeless, Respondent Number 19 said he didn't know, as he didn't pay any attention to it.

He said that his perception of the way the media cover the homeless had not changed since becoming homeless and that he was unaware of what a healthy way would be for the media to cover the homeless.

When asked if he had an opinion on the matter, Respondent Number 19 said, "No matter what I say, they're gonna treat it the same way anyway (and) … just brush it under the carpet most of the time, or say that it's a big problem."

This respondent thought that the average person in Albuquerque probably gets most of his or her information about the homeless from the (broadcast) news or the newspaper. However, he was unable to offer an opinion as to where reporters get their information about the homeless from.

Regarding the advice he would give to media heads about how they could improve their coverage of the homeless, Number 19 said, "I'd tell them to stay down in the shelter for awhile themselves and do everything that everybody else has to. (Get a) first-hand experience look at it."

The following interviews were conducted by me with individuals who were not staying at Joy Junction.

Respondent Number 20

Asked where he was living at the time of the interview, Number 20 said, "I've lived in the camp, at a shelter, and when money's available, I'll pitch in for a room." He said that, in his opinion, the media's coverage of the homeless both locally and nationally has been "pretty negative, there's been nothing said positive about it."

According to this respondent, "Every little petty crime that's ever been done in Albuquerque seems to be put back onto the homeless. It seems like the lack of bus services is back onto the homeless. I mean, everything's blamed on the homeless. That's the way I feel, and I think that's the way the majority of the homeless people feel, sort of putting 'em in a very stressful situation. They feel like they're not wanted, and most of the time we aren't wanted."

Had his perception of the way the media cover the homeless had changed since he became homeless. He replied, "It hasn't changed per se, like I'm more bitter towards them, but it seems there hasn't been anything ... it's more or less a media hype-up. They want to go ahead and say that because of this one incident, it's the homeless. They place more blame on the homeless always ... My perception has been there, but it's always been negative," he said.

Regarding what he thought would be a healthier way for the media to cover the homeless he said, "For them to go ahead and give the homeless person, or someone responsible for the homeless person, an assignment and say there are some good sides. I'm not sure if it can be documented, but people do leave one another's personal possessions alone, if they find it out on the street or in a park area, they realize it belongs to someone else, let's leave it alone. There's always that little one percent element, the criminal mind, that says, 'hey, let's go destroy it!' There'll always be someone like that, whether they're homeless or not."

When asked how he thought the average person in Albuquerque got most of his or her information about the homeless, Number 20 said he thought they got it from the media, and then he explained how different things can be for the homeless.

"Whereas being homeless, one day if you're lucky to catch a TV, if you're lucky enough to get a current daily paper," he said. "Otherwise you don't hear about it until a week later, or three or four days later."

Number 20 said he thought that the media get their information about the homeless from "their main files ... 'Cause I don't see no reporters out here unless they're in disguise," he said. "That's pretty obvious, 'cause I've been on the street here for three years. That's not something I'm proud of, but

I'm getting to know a lot of people. People are starting to get to know me by my first name. That's sort like saying, 'I've been here too long; that's a little bit too long for me.'"

Respondent Number 21

Respondent Number 21, a Native American, said he that became homeless through a marital break up and lack of employment. "I'm off the reservation, there's a lack of employment back on the reservation, and I came here in Albuquerque five years ago," he said. "I done fairly well here, I got my own apartment; then being in this city has its influences, not just only from the media but from outside influences that sort of affected me."

What would he say if he was invited to a meeting of media heads in Albuquerque and asked to suggest how media coverage of the homeless could be improved? He said, "The best way they can start is by integrating the reporters down to this level," he said. "Right now we have people that are basically ... big outlets. First thing we see are these big helicopters and that sort of puts a distance between one another. Then we see the reporters, and then there's nothing wrong with being dressed, but then they give us this distinct classification. 'Hey, this guy's unemployed,' but being homeless, we've been wearing the same clothes that we had three days ago ... We need someone from the homeless that's here from the homeless to go ahead and gather the data and report it."

Number 21 said that the news media have preconceived ideas about the homeless. "They sort of have a mind set of, 'yeah, they're homeless and they're criminals, and drug dealers' and all that, whereas most main problem is unemployment, lack of jobs, and right now we have this thing in the Middle East and people have relatives out there," he said. "And that sort of puts a strain on them, they can't get to a phone and they can't get in touch with people through the postal services and things like that."

Respondent Number 22

Respondent Number 22 alternated between living on the street, homeless shelters and the West Side Jail, a temporary emergency homeless shelter.

When asked what he thought about the media's coverage of the homeless, he said that he used to believe the media portrayed the homeless as second class citizens. "When I used to be a taxpayer, and I try to be a taxpayer every chance I get, I'm no different than the average person that works," he said. "I used to drive trucks; I used to do construction; I used to do all kinds of things. Whatever I could do to make a dollar, but at the same time, you know, a lot of people look at me and a few other people I know, and they frown, as though we shouldn't be in their presence. It kind of makes me feel inadequate."

Respondent Number 22 replied that that his perception of the way the media cover the homeless had changed somewhat since he himself became homeless. "Sometime they may throw in a good word or a good notion," he said. "That makes you think that there might be some hope that people might change their mind, because it's in the media. The media influence other people to treat you kind of bad, you know."

Prior to becoming homeless, this respondent said that his impression of the way the media cover the homeless was "mediocre."

Following up on that thought, Number 22 said a better way for the media to cover the homeless would be to personally "confront" them.

"The media could possibly help a lot of people not to be homeless by exposing some programs that could help homeless people no longer be homeless, at least get them off the streets," he said. "That's one step closer to finding a job, or doing something productive, and possibly straightening their lives out."

Regarding how he thought the average person in Albuquerque got most of his or her knowledge about the homeless, Number 22 said, "More or less by word of mouth, from friends, and partially from the media," he said. "The information they get from the media is entirely different from the version they get from word of mouth. The word of mouth, you know how good news travels fast, well word of mouth people know personally just how a homeless person struggles and what they go through. The media, they're just there 10 or 15 minutes, and they have no idea. Once they turn their camera and their lights off, the homeless still have a life to live."

To the question about where he thought a typical reporter gets most of his or her knowledge about the homeless, he said that a reporter can go to homeless shelters, because "naturally the best place to get it is from a homeless person."

Respondent Number 22 said that if he was invited to a meeting of media executives and given the chance to offer insight about how the media could improve their coverage of the homeless, he would tell them not to begin with a negative attitude. "Step to the situation with an open mind, because not every homeless person is in the same situation as the next homeless person," he said. "When you step to a homeless person and you speak negative toward them, you're going to get a negative response. You step up to a homeless person and you don't have to have a sympathetic ear, or have a sympathetic heart. Have a sympathetic well being, so to speak and try to see eye-to-eye with that person, because you never know if you're in that situation what you're looking at."

It would also be helpful, Number 22 said, if in addition to interviewing homeless people singly, the media would conduct group interviews. "It's okay to talk to one at a time, because you're gonna get a better idea, but when you talk to a group of people at one time, you're gonna get a better sense of what the need is for that particular group, " he said.

Respondent Number 23

Respondent Number 23 said he moved to Albuquerque from Denver because of the warmer climate and what he hoped would be a better employment situation. However, he was living at the West Side Jail Emergency Shelter at the time of the interview and had been there for about 35 days.

Asked what he thought of the media's coverage of the homeless, he responded quickly. "I consider the media more or less does what the government wants, and they want to use us homeless people as people who do drugs, lazy, and it's far from that. If you're homeless and lazy, you'll starve and freeze," he said. "As far as the media goes, you're dealing with people who are above the normal and they don't want to rock the boat as far as the government. They don't want to let the true message out, the truth about the homeless. It's just better to push them to the side, consider them drug addicts or lazy people. And as far as me, I'm not a drug addict and I'm not lazy. I have a disability but I just moved to the city – I'm from Denver – and I'm slowly trying to get some affordable housing and get back into work. I work through a labor pool, and it's just hard with the economy like this."

Had his perception of the way the media cover the homeless had changed since he himself had become homeless? He replied, "I was raised never to judge a person, just because you're better off than the next person. But as far as the media, they're consistent as far as viewing the homeless people or any area of people that most of society don't like to see. They've always looked at homeless people as drug addicts or lazy people."

With regard to his opinion, as expressed in his answer, about a better way for the media to cover the homeless, it was apparent that he wanted the media to advocate for the homeless. He suggested that the homeless would be good employees and not lazy, although he indicated that some of them have mental problems and need help. "And maybe if they covered the real story of people that were homeless, maybe that would touch other people, instead of showing the negativity of the homeless," he said. "A lot of veterans are homeless. They don't show that there are lots of homeless people who were very successful, and in some part of their life something went wrong. And they show a general stand-back picture of it, people looking grubby or grimy or asking for something. It's a personal thing, if they got more in touch with the people themselves, then the public would see that homeless people are real people."

This respondent also said he felt that the media spend too much time covering the homeless agencies and not enough time directly filming the homeless. "Some of these agencies, if they (the media) would interview the people as individuals, they would see that some of the agencies aren't really helping people the way they should. A lot of money goes to them and they're used for staff," he said.

How did he think the average person in Albuquerque gets most of his or her knowledge about the homeless? He believed the information comes from television. "And they might drive by and see homeless in lines at certain places, so they know that's for homeless people. I would say in Albuquerque, the general working public, 95% of the information they get is from television coverage."

Asked how the average reporter gets most of his or her information about the homeless, Respondent Number 23 said he had not seen many reporters actually interviewing the homeless. "They'll go by and interview the director or a person who's running the shelter, and I guess talk to the police," he said. "If they would take the time to talk to homeless individuals, you would that each one has a different story, but also each one needs help in a different area."

When asked how the media could improve their coverage of the homeless, this respondent reiterated that, in his opinion, the media needed to talk to the homeless. "Agencies help, but if you talk to the person that's homeless, you'll know exactly why he's homeless, what he needs ... A lot of homeless people are victims. Victims of the system, and they should show that, and they're victims of the police. They don't want to show that."

Respondent Number 23 continued his refrain. "But a cop stops somebody homeless, he thinks he has the right to say, 'empty your pockets' ... and that's why the media should be more talking to the individuals, than going on hearsay and stats and statistics, which really don't show nothing. There's no way to really count the homeless. The best way to count the homeless is to ask another homeless person, ask 'how many people do you think are out here?' They know."

Respondent Number 24

Respondent Number 24 failed to answer the question about how the media cover the homeless. Instead he said, "I think winter makes it worse. Summer bring migrants, immigrants, but the homeless, we should take care of our own, because there are a lot of people out there out of work. But for the homeless, there are a few to help somebody out, because a lot of employers would rather pay less for migrants than for an American, because an American wants more money and a migrant will take whatever he wants."

Asked how he thought the average person in Albuquerque gets most of his or her knowledge about the homeless, Number 24 said from the homeless. Continuing, he said, "I just met someone yesterday, a regular civilian, who asked me where he could get something to eat because he was hungry."

How did he think the average reporter got most of his or her knowledge about the homeless? In a rambling answer he said, "If he asks a rich person or someone who doesn't know about it because they haven't been out here, you know what, I've been there. I used to shun them off. But now I'm one of the shunned. Never think about it that way, do you? It happens to somebody else, but until it happens to you."

Regarding what he would say if invited to a meeting of media executives and asked how the media could improve their coverage of the homeless, Number 24 said, "My dad, if he were alive, he'd tell me run for governor. If they had a meeting at the convention center, I would take them on the routes. I would take them from the lower valley to the west side, even to the heights; they have people living under bridges. I'd take them with night cameras to see how they live. To see how we survive out here. That's how the world will know. And it is hard. I'm just a survivor, that's all I am."

Continuing, he said "They don't put enough in the newspapers, you don't see them in the head covers, but you see war, and famine, and American aid to the rest of the world, but where the (expletive) are we standing at? They don't even see what's happening in America, but yet we give aid to the rest of the (expletive) starving countries? What are we doing here? That Hubble telescope that broke, why do we want to see what's going on across the universe when we can't even see what's going on here on earth? Should I run for governor, senator, president? I went to the University of California at Berkeley? Does it matter to the (expletive) public what kind of mind I got? They don't see it that way. I need an application, I need references, I need this and that, I got it all. But they look at a homeless person and they won't even hire him."

Respondent Number 25

When Respondent Number 25 was asked where he lived he said, "I live in a camp, my own camp," he said, "so police don't throw all my stuff away, I keep it hidden from them and from everybody else so I don't get robbed … It's not too far from here. I try to stay at a low profile, but I don't believe in what is going on around here."

Regarding what he thought about the media's coverage of the homeless both locally and nationally, Number 25 said he hadn't seen that much, with a few exceptions. "Except when the mayor and the police are trying to arrest people for panhandling to get certain types of money to pay for their medicines or their bus tickets or a meal or two," he said. He continued, "The media don't cover the homeless too much. The only time they do cover us is when someone is hurt or killed, like ... one of the homeless guys was run over by a semi when it was backing up to deliver its goods. Now that was a tragic accident. Like Saturday ... (when) we had media over because the police kicked everybody out of the park. The media took and covered what was going on. That was just one station that was doing the covering, just one station. Station 13. There should have been more than just one. A lot of people turn their backs on the homeless. I guess they've got a policy of 'out of sight, out of mind.'"

Had his perception of the way the media cover the homeless had changed since he became homeless. Number 25 said that it had, and that he did feel the homeless are not being terribly "well presented" by the media. "The media is not out searching to find out what's going on and why it's going on," he said. "I don't think everybody understands that a lot (of) the homeless ... have problems, and then there's some that don't have problems. But those that are willing to work and go out, need a special type of education. Some type of training to help them. A lot of the homeless would like that training. And then you have those that are handicapped and can't work, and are on Social Security. Social Security's not enough to pay for their rent, so if they can't pay for their rent, where are they gonna live? Out on the street.

"A healthier way for the media to cover the homeless," this respondent said, would for them to be "more understanding" and to "go out and see what is going on. Ask questions; find out why one person's homeless, why he wants to live that way," he said. "A lot of people don't even trust our own government or their own city. Especially when they outlaw panhandling and try to make it against the law to be homeless. In the 30's, there was no law about homeless, because of the Great Depression. Look what's going on right now ... maybe we're going back into another Great Depression. Nobody's even thought of that."

How did Respondent Number 25 think the average person in Albuquerque obtained most of his or her knowledge about the homeless? "From the police or a store owner," he said. "They don't like the way somebody looks, because of the way they look, they're automatically pinned as a homeless ... or they're driving down the street and they see us walking down the street.

The opinions are just like that. We had opinions of other ethnic groups and stuff like that, through how we grew up. Some of them perceive it like that, how mom and dad tells them this, and so they take it as they grow up."

Number 25 related a recent experience. "I went to use the restrooms because I had my coat on and these on, and I am homeless. Public restroom is for the public, not just certain people, not for the rich or the government or anything. Public restrooms are for public people. Because I was homeless, I was told to go somewhere else to go to the bathroom."

This individual was unsure how the average reporter gets his or her information about the homeless, but he did offer some thoughts. "I think they get most of their information from police reports that the police write up every night after they get done with their shifts. They drive around and see us on the streets, but they don't stop and talk to us. They don't stop and visit with us. People don't understand what's going on," he said.

"I was homeless, not by my own device, but because of my sister's landlord telling her he didn't want me in the house, so I became homeless," he elaborated. "I am trying to find another way to go get my stuff; I got tents and stuff. I'm going to put them up and live in them. That's my home. I got a bike, I can get around. But as long as people are taking and terrorizing people, or turning their backs and not wanting to find out what's ticking, or not wanting to help, then people are not gonna ever find out what's wrong with the system. There's something wrong with the system, because we got so many people that are homeless."

If asked by the media how they could improve their coverage of the homeless, Respondent Number 25 said he would tell them to visit with the homeless more often and see what is really going on. "Find out if we need medical. Find out what kind of education we need to get out of this mess," he said. "Find out if the state can help us get a home. We're a minority. Nobody wants to look at us, out of sight, out of mind, like I say. Nobody wants to see us. We're a thorn in their side, actually."

Because of that, this respondent said, the media "don't really want to do too much of an interview with us. They see us as trying to play on people's sympathy. I don't want charity. I just want help. If we had an education to where we could set up to get out of a mess, or any type of help like a house, the tools to get us a job, something that we can do something with.

That would help us a lot. People don't realize that we're not insects; we're not rodents; we're not vomit. We're human beings. Isn't it that we're supposed to help each other out? That's what it says in the Bible. We're all Christians, and yet all the Christians that say they're Christians, turn their backs on everybody. And that's not right."

Respondent Number 26

The next respondent said he had lived outside, in a camp, for six years.

Concerning what Respondent Number 26 thought of the media's coverage of the homeless, he said he usually tries to stay away from the media. "Most of the time, it's just like one-sided I believe. It's like a procedure, they go down there, their own highway," he said. "Just having a set of rules they have to follow to get funding. I think it's one-sided. It's like any journalist, things get edited out, and out of context." A more healthy way for the media to cover the homeless, this respondent said, would be by "better journalism … Just listen to the replies."

Number 26 initially said he did not know how the average reporter gets most of his or her knowledge about the homeless. However, he then added, "Most of it from seeing the council meetings; get input from the outside."

Asked how the media could improve their coverage of the homeless, he said they needed to "tag along" with a couple of people.

Respondent Number 27

Respondent Number 27 said he had been living on the street and in the West Side (old jail) shelter. He said he has been homeless on and off for about four years. Disability and lack of work resulted in his homelessness, he said. This respondent said that his disability stopped him from working at his trade as an aircraft technician, and that after moving to New Mexico, his third marriage dissolved "and things just went downhill."

The respondent said that the media give a false interpretation of who the homeless really are. "They look at us as being degenerate and downcast, and just a problem to society," he said. "What they don't realize is that the average 9–5 person working is one paycheck away from being where we're at. The system of society, the economic structure of the U.S., is not designed to help the homeless, it's designed to keep 'em on that level."

This respondent said that his perception of the way the media cover the homeless has worsened since he himself became homeless. "When I was working and had a home, I looked at the media coverage as being one-sided, but now that I'm homeless, I think the media coverage is even worse," he said. "One-sided because they seem to be blaming the homeless for everything, and looking at them, trying to cover them up and hide them, get rid of them. And if anything happens, it's the homeless this, the homeless that, saying that the majority of the homeless are alcoholics and drug addicts, when actually, statistically, 85% of all addicts and alcoholics are people that are working 9–5."

Respondent Number 27 suggested that a healthier way for the media to cover the homeless would be to "come down and find out what really goes on, and how and why these people are homeless, and why there is nothing really being done to help the homeless get on their feet. But they don't even look at that."

He thought that the average person in Albuquerque gets most of his or her knowledge about the homeless from the media. "And I think that it's one sided. What I feel the average American person needs to do is to come down here and spend a week with the homeless and find out what it's really about, and then they will see for themselves what's going on."

Asked what he meant by a "one-sided picture," Respondent Number 27 said, "Is that they are blaming homelessness on the homeless people, blaming everything on them, that they don't want to do anything, that they're lazy, they're alcoholics, and really it's just the opposite."

While this respondent was unaware how the average reporter gets his or her knowledge about the homeless, he did state that the information being reported "is not real. I was down last Saturday when they were harassing Brother Ralph (a local homeless activist), and here's a man who devotes his life to helping the homeless, giving out food, clothes and everything else, and he's banned from a public park to feed the homeless," he said. "You can't feed anybody here. Because there was some guy that was harassing him, saying he was cast from the devil. And the media went straight to this guy, and now they're blaming Brother Ralph for all this other stuff."

What would Number 27 say if he was invited to a meeting of media heads in Albuquerque and asked how the media could improve their coverage of the homeless. He said, "I would tell them to come down and spend a week homeless. Go through what we go through, and then report that."

This respondent said that he was unaware that the local CBS affiliate had done just that about six months prior to his interview with me. He said that he was aware of a number of disabled homeless individuals. "Here's people in wheel chairs, crutches, one-legged, I mean, mentally, physically." However, he said that he had never seen a story about the disabled homeless.

Respondent Number 28

Respondent Number 28 had been staying at the local Salvation Army Women's Center for about eight months, even though there is usually a time limit of three months.

However, she said that the agency did not like her. "They've given me a week to find a job or I'm out of there. I had a job before Christmas, but I had to quit because I was really (physically) ill."

When asked what she thought of the media's coverage of the homeless, there was a long silence. An individual from the Albuquerque Homeless Coalition, who had helped set up these interviews, asked, "Do you think you're portrayed accurately? Do you read the paper about the homeless and about them getting arrested for trespassing?"

She replied, "No, I disapprove of the way the police are handling the homeless, and being abused."

Asked how the media reports that issue, Respondent Number 28 said, "They don't really, they discriminate against us … They don't want us to be like the taxpayer people. They don't think we deserve anything."

She said that homeless single women need more help. When asked how the media could help with that, she said that the media could, "Help us find a place to live, help us get jobs."

When asked how she thought the average person in Albuquerque gets most of his or her information about the homeless, Respondent Number 28 said that she thought they relied on their own opinion. She was initially unable to substantiate that statement any further, but then said that she thought their opinions were based on reading the papers, from seeing panhandlers and homeless people out on the streets.

Regarding how she thought the average reporter got most of his or her information about the homeless, this respondent said "They arrive at the scene, I guess. That's the only thing I can think of … I would assume that's the only way they're gonna get that information is if they're at the scene of the crime."

Respondent Number 28 said that she did not know what she would tell the media if asked to express her opinion about how the media could improve their coverage of the homeless.

Respondent Number 29

Respondent Number 29 was also staying at the Salvation Army Women's Center. She had been there for two months.

Regarding her opinion about the way the media cover the homeless, she said, "They seem to care when somebody speaks up, but actually they don't do that much coverage like they should."

This respondent said that her perception of the way the media cover the homeless had not changed since she herself became homeless.

How did she feel the media could better cover the homeless? "I think they should get in there. Be one of us. Go to a shelter, stay there, see what it's like, what it feels like," she said. She too was unaware that the local CBS affiliate had done that about six months prior to the interview.

This respondent said that as a homeless person, she felt "degraded" by people. She was asked if she felt people degraded her because of the way the homeless are portrayed by the media. She agreed, but qualified it by saying "but not everybody's the same. I can only speak for myself."

Concerning how the average person in Albuquerque gets most of his or her knowledge about the homeless, she thought that it was most probably from the streets and by seeing homeless people. "We do see a lot of bad reports in the media, like a lot of us homeless people could do a lot better, so we won't be getting the bad rap. Because that's what it basically boils down to. We're put down because of just one bad apple in the tree, you know," she said.

She addressed a recent incident concerning a meal provider feeding meals to the homeless in a local park. However, he was apparently closed down by city officials because he lacked the proper licensing requirements from the health department. Respondent Number 29 said she was there at the park when the incident occurred and the media turned up. "When the media turned up, there was a couple of people that spoke up … They were talking about that they were getting hassled for giving the homeless food and clothes, they only wanted to make sure that the homeless ate and got dressed. And I seen for myself," she said, "because I've gone there myself, you know they leave that park really clean and empty afterwards. They're just getting a bad rap for the simple reason that, it would be different if they left the park all dirty or whatever, but … the park is (always) made clean after the food is served." She also thought that because the local CBS affiliate was there early on in the incident (apparently the only local network news affiliate in attendance) that the station had been tipped off.

How did she think the typical reporter gets most of his or her knowledge about the homeless? Referring to the incident in the park she said, "From tips. The news was there because one of the gentlemen that goes there all the time, he's the one that called. They had a scheduled meeting and that's when everything went down. They weren't able to go to the park with food in the vehicles or anything like that."

Asked what she would tell media heads if invited to comment on how the media could improve their coverage of the homeless, she said that she would tell them not to focus on all the bad publicity the homeless have received. "They really need to look into it in depth, so they can know exactly what we're going through, or what that person is going through, in order for them to really know," this respondent said. "It's like, a lot of them don't know because they haven't gone through it, but they don't know, they could possibly go through it one day. They think it could never happen to them. And maybe until that happens, they won't know."

Respondent Number 29 said that she would like to see better communication between the media and the homeless. "It works both ways, you know," she said. "Like at one point, the interviews over there, they caught people drinking in the park. They already know that this is not (typical). We're all gonna lose out for just a few people."

Respondent Number 30

According to this respondent, he was living in "A camp. Not too far from here. I live in a building." He said he reads Albuquerque's morning paper daily but watched television news infrequently.

He suggested that, in his opinion, media coverage of the homeless was negative. "Just negative; the homeless people are a nuisance," he explained. "I don't think the media understands that the majority of the homeless people don't want to be homeless; it's just the situation that they're in. Sometimes they stay homeless, and sometimes they get off the street. It just depends on the individual. The ones that are trying is the ones that the media makes it hard for them." Just how do the media "make it hard" for the homeless? "Because they think the ones that aren't trying, is negative, and the ones that are, and then they think that everybody's not trying to get off the street," Respondent Number 30 said.

However, this respondent was unable to cite specific instances of negative portrayals of the homeless in Albuquerque. However, in Oklahoma, he said, the situation is "terrible. In Oklahoma, if you even have a backpack, the cops will stop you. If you have a backpack walking downtown, you'll get stopped for no reason at all," he claimed.

He said that media coverage of those incidents influences the way that people think about the homeless by causing them to be afraid.

Respondent Number 30 said that his perception of the way the media cover the homeless has always been negative; that the media have always covered the homeless badly.

Respondent Number 31

Respondent Number 31, homeless for 10 years, four times in Oregon and "the fifth time down here by choice," identified himself as being both "houseless and camping."

Asked why he was homeless "by choice," he said, "I knew I wouldn't make it any other way."

This respondent said that media coverage of the homeless tends to identify them as "outcasts and do everything they can to move us out of the city." He claimed that the police also feel the same way, and that the media and the police influence each other. He said that his perception of the way the media cover the homeless had not changed since he became homeless.

Could he suggest how the media could better cover the homeless? Respondent Number 31 replied, "I think all cops and media and counselors need to take a 30-day course in Homeless 101. Just live out there with just the clothes on their back and find out how hard it is, with sore feet and knees and backs and arms, to get from point A to point B. If they have to, learn how to panhandle or pick stuff up off the ground to make ends meet. (They should) live there themselves and see for themselves what it really takes to find a warm spot where you're not gonna be harassed by the police department."

Respondent Number 31 said that the average person in Albuquerque gets his information about the homeless from a variety of sources. "From friends that have seen a homeless person and they derive their own what they think is good or bad, whether it is right or wrong, they choose to perceive it this way or that way ... Media plays a part in it. The cops play a part in it. The mayor plays a lot in it," he said.

According to this respondent, reporters learn about the homeless from whoever they are talking to. "And if whoever (they're) talking to is not a homeless, then (they) gets a picture painted by that person as to how that person perceives the homeless to be."

"Media heads need to know something about the homeless," Respondent Number 31 said. "That we are human just like them. We may not have the house and the cars and the clothes to show ourselves as successful business men and women, but we do have knowledge that is gained only by the streets and can help them learn to do things (like) watch the traffic at night. We see what goes on (and) what people do."

Appendix D
Ethnographic Field Research
Introduction

This pilot study field research was conducted in advance of the actual field work for the book, and was an attempt to observe the actions of guests staying at Joy Junction homeless shelter in Albuquerque, New Mexico.

I felt that the following observation provided an informative snapshot of the behavior of homeless people at a shelter who were not aware they were being observed.

Methodology

I was as unobtrusive as possible while observing guest activities. I accomplished this by looking out of the main office door at the activities occurring in the main building of the shelter. Because guests were used to seeing him briefly observe activities on a daily basis, the results no doubt reflect an accurate representation of typical activities occurring at Joy Junction during these times.

The field work was done at various times throughout the day over the course of two weeks.

Observation

It is 3.20 p.m. on Feb. 25 2002 on a relatively calm Sunday afternoon in the main building of Joy Junction, Albuquerque's largest emergency homeless shelter, where I am the founder and executive director.

Holding a baby, a pregnant member of the shelter's life skills program (called the Christ in Power Program and referred to by the acronym CIPP) is distraught about the recent abandonment of five children at Joy Junction. She says, "I just want to go out and find that woman. But my husband says 'Maybe she was suicidal so perhaps the kids are in a better place.' I ponder briefly the vastly different reaction to the abandonment.

A man who has physical and mental problems, staggers into the office and says, "I hate Channel four, (the Albuquerque NBC affiliate)." A participant in the shelter's life skills program asks why and the man responds, "Because they always cut out."

Just as the man is staggering out of the office, a Joy Junction parking lot attendant comes in. He is dressed in a plaid shirt with a blue undershirt and blue jeans with hair sticking up and asks the Joy Junction pastoral counselor, "That girl you had at the movies. Was she 18?"

"No, she was in her mid 50's," responds the counselor.

"Okay, just trying to scare you," says the parking lot attendant. That is typical humor at Joy Junction. Everyone deals on a consistent basis with so much heartbreak and desperation that sometimes the humor goes beyond humorous to plain silly and sometimes almost degenerates into the plain bizarre. I understand it is a coping mechanism that often manifests in situations like ours.

It is now 3:25 p.m., and about a dozen people are quietly sitting around Joy Junction's multi-purpose building, some at tables reading and others on couches. A man is in the CIPP office asking questions – maybe translating – in Spanish. A man is leaning over the walker of the individual with physical and mental problems joking with him, while the sound of a baby's loud crying fills the multi, as the staff refers to the building.

After several minutes of the baby's crying growing progressively louder, the CIPP person on duty asks the parent of the crying baby, "Can you take him to another part of the multi? I can't hear what's going on here." I think that would be a pretty typical reaction anywhere.

Although it is a typically fairly slow Sunday at the shelter, all these situations going on serve to remind me that there is nonetheless a busy undercurrent of activity.

A few minutes later, I hear parts of what is sadly a fairly typical shelter conversation drifting out of the CIPP office. "He drinks too much and he's already hit her." While this conversation is going on in the small CIPP office, a small baby is on the floor playing. A young boy pushing a stroller around the building almost runs the baby over. He is told to stop. I think that in every place where you have children, they always end up playing and in about as many places, they are usually told to stop.

It is now 4:30 p.m., and the multi is filled with people eating the evening meal. (Dinner on Sunday is from 4 p.m. to 5 p.m.). Most people are sitting down eating their evening meal off institutional type trays but about a dozen or so are still standing in the serving line. There is not much audible conversation going on from my fairly unobtrusive listening post a few feet away, just a few laughs here and there.

I can only see one person who is not eating. An elderly black woman with graying hair is sitting quietly on a couch just a few feet from the office where I am listening. For the most part, she is staring vacantly into mid-air. She typifies the stereotypical image that many people have of the homeless.

The overall atmosphere resembles a busy, well-ordered and well-structured beehive with lots going on. While it appears (to me, anyway) to be a comforting, reassuring environment, I wonder if that comfort I feel is because of my familiarity with the environment. I wonder how many of the scores of people I can see eating dinner are as comfortable with it as I am.

By 5:10 p.m., supper is over and all the tables have been stacked to one side to make way for the upcoming church service. The Joy Junction staff chaplain is helping set up the equipment, bongo drums, electric piano, etc. As a faith-based ministry, church services and Bible studies form a core part of what Joy Junction is all about.

I hear another snatch of conversation coming out of the CIPP office. Someone says, "All you had to do was answer the question." Another person answers, "Tough it out."

The first individual responds, "I'm tired."

Minutes later, two tall men begin their after-dinner chores of methodically sweeping and mopping the multi floor prior to the chairs being put back down for church. Daily chores are required as a condition for staying at the shelter. Continued refusal to do chores will eventually result in a person being asked to leave the shelter. Doing chores is all about trying to inculcate in these folk some measure of responsibility and to help them make a successful transition back to the real world.

The black woman is still sitting in the same place. The only difference about her now is that she has a soft-covered Bible balanced on her lap. Now about a dozen people are sitting on couches that line the perimeter of the multi building. Nobody is reading. Most people are just looking. That is another typical homeless profile.

A short time later, a kitchen worker who is on the program drops off lunches in the CIPP office refrigerator for the graveyard shift. I ask him if he is behaving. He responds, "Yea, I was just dropping off lunches. See, I've stacked them nice and neat." He is aware of who I am and anxious to please.

The kitchen worker disappears from sight and a man comes by and stops at the office right in front of my listening post. How is he doing? He says, "Not so good."

I ask him why and he says that because he has just broken up with his girlfriend, his stay at Joy Junction has now reverted to overnight status. He is disappointed and says, "I had a lot of plans. I had a lot I could do for this place. See these three couches? That's what I used to do for my business – fix them."

I utter condolences to the effect of, "Yea, that's what happens." I don't know if he knew my position at Joy Junction.

He responds, "Rules are rules," and walks off. I believe that this is the man who has been earlier accused by his girlfriend of beating her up. Even after having helped the homeless for 20 years and thinking that nothing new is ever going to surprise me, I am still pretty astounded at this incident. This man is more concerned about his inability to fix the shelter's couches than he is about the welfare of his (now previous) girlfriend.

While this conversation is going on, the band for the evening service is getting set up. People continue to sit.

At 5:35 p.m., with the chores being completed, chairs are being now put back on the floor for the evening service, and the sound system is in the final stages of set up.

At 5.40 p.m., with the sound system now in place, the band is strumming and tuning up prior to the start of the Sunday 6 p.m. service. A handful of people are sitting in the bright-colored orange and yellow chairs waiting for the service to begin. A smiling African-American woman waves to me and points to the baby she has cradled in her lap. The pastor makes some apparent last minute adjustments to the sound system. A number of people are sitting around on couches.

It's now 6 p.m. and the worship portion of the church service begins. Shelter guests sing, "Sing a joyful song unto the Lord; praise the Lord with gladness because He alone is God." There is a small amount of slow clapping going on. Seventeen people are standing up, about 15% of the entire crowd. I am struck by the fact that most of those singing here tonight do not have a home, but despite that they are still able to sing and worship the Lord. There's happy singing in the midst of homeless despair. That almost seems like an oxymoron, but a scene similar to this one is duplicated in hundreds of gospel rescue missions across the country.

While the singing is going on, a man at the back of the multi stands supported by a walker looking on. Just behind him in the entrance to the multi building is a shopping cart piled high with clean bed linens ready to be put away in the linen closet. I am struck by the contrast of such a "normal" church service occurring at the front of the building, with a scene from a "normal" homeless environment occurring at the back.

The next day, Feb. 26 2002, I continue my watch. It is 7:55 a.m. and very quiet in the multi-purpose building. There are just two people sitting around on chairs.

A woman comes up to my listening post and says to me (I do not know whether she knows who I am), "I was in bed for 30 days with the flu. My doctor years ago in Arkansas gave me a little blue pill which had no side effects. I had to take it every day. It was just an allergy tablet. It's allergies. I was just born with that retraction. Some of the people here really don't care. Their brains still race. I just wanna get rid of these sinus sniffles. It's been an infection."

She stops for a moment and I look across the multi where a man is slowly and methodically mopping the floor. The woman continues talking and says, "Spanish people, they talk so fast, amigo, amigo. Four years of it – I beg their pardon. You think they talk slow. They don't."

Suddenly, she changes her conversational track and says, "You ever been down to 'La Jumbo Fish, crawfish pie?' Why is it so important to remember the names of songs these days?"

The woman wanders off but returns quickly with a purposeful walk. She starts talking again. "Did they ever cure whiplash? I was in a vehicle accident in East Texas. I was a passenger and impacted by an eighteen-wheeler (truck.)

What do you have to do to get a neck brace? Go in the ER?" She puts her hand on the back of her neck and wanders off again. It is quickly apparent to me that she is apparently pretty seriously mentally ill and taking that into consideration, her conversation is not terribly outlandish. I have heard worse during the approximately 20 years I have worked with New Mexico's homeless.

At 9:40 a.m., it is still very quiet in the multi. Two boys are walking around the multi aimlessly. One of them is swinging some socks. Four people are sitting at the table talking. A lady is sitting at a couch, busily engrossed in something.

I hear conversation coming from the CIPP office. Someone says, "Michael is going to be upset when he gets home."

Someone else says, "I seem to have no eyesight when I first wake up. I just can't find it." I am again struck by the humor that is exhibited both by guests and staff at Joy Junction. It really is an indispensable part of keeping perspective when living and working in such a crisis-oriented environment.

I am startled out of my reverie when my name is mentioned by somebody and a lady turns around to face me. "Hi, Jeremy. I didn't know you were Jeremy." She walks off without saying anything else.

There are now six people in the multi. A woman is sitting on the couch with her suitcase in front of her.

A CIPP program participant walking by the office says to everyone (and no one in particular), "I'm sending people to the thrift store and it's not even open." Even though there is a considerable amount of humor in evidence at the shelter, there is also some frustration, and sometimes I realize that we as administrators and managers may fail to let those under us know what is open and closed and just what is going on at the shelter.

I take a break from my observation and resume at 1:00 p.m. when the lady is still sitting on the couch with her suitcase in front of her. A woman who, I suspect, is younger than she looks comes to the office door talking to herself. She says nothing in particular, puts her hand on her stomach and moves away. There are now five people in the multi building.

On March 8 at 3:35 p.m., there are three people sitting in the multi and two sitting outside the CIPP office. It is all very quiet. A staff member comes to the office and says, "There's a (Bernalillo) County car parked out there. Do you want me to check and see what's going on?" I give permission.

Ten minutes later, the staff person comes in to let me know that she has spoken to the county official. He told her he was checking on the foundations for our newly-donated motel buildings in reference to our request for an amended site plan.

At 4:00 p.m., there are two people in the multi. A very talkative man wearing a wide-brimmed hat comes to the office looking for a worker (or workers – I am unable to determine which). He tells the staff person, "I'm looking for someone to work. I'm an early bird. I'm 56 years old and I've already busted two sledgehammers today. I don't believe in working them for just a few minutes. I'm talking about seven or eight hours work. I'll pay them and then have enough money left over to run my business as well."

The staff person listens and says that there is no one available at the moment, but she will announce the job at supper as that is the best time. The man hands her a sheet of paper with contact information and leaves looking happy.

At 4:15 p.m., a woman calls and asks if she and her children can come and stay at the shelter. She and her husband have stayed with us some years back at the shelter and she has worked for us in the office quite recently. We had thought that they were really back on their feet again.

I learn that this former guest's husband has quit his job against the advice of his pastor and wife, and for the last three weeks or so has spent the time (when he should have been working) being "spiritual." While his wife is working at home, he has been discussing the nuances of Bible prophecy with his sister. (The sister, who is recovering from a car accident, is staying with the couple while she recuperates).

The woman tells me that the situation is too much for her to handle. She has told her husband this morning she doesn't care what he does or how much he earns (two cents an hour would be fine), but he needs to get a job and give her some 'space' for eight hours a day. Apparently the husband gets mad and hits his wife, who leaves. She tells me that she had told him once before that if he ever hit her again that she would leave. (The implication is that the last time he hit her was a long time ago).

We offer the woman and her three children a place to stay. As they are preparing to check in, I hear her gratefully exclaim, "Thank God that at least we've got a place to stay!"

"Where?" asks the youngest of her three children. "Right here, says the woman, pointing to a couch before it was decided that they would be given a room.

"Weird, very weird." says the little girl while she is clutching a donated stuffed animal. While she doesn't realize how humorous she sounds, she has definitely brought a much lighter feeling to a very tense situation.

At 4:45 p.m., the multi is filling up in anticipation of the 5 p.m. evening meal. The woman's children are sitting on a couch talking to our children's ministry supervisor while their mom is getting signed in. A long-time staff member tells the woman, "Give yourself time to relax. Do you remember how it was the first time you were here?" I thank God for our children's ministry supervisor, who has been with Joy Junction since about the third week we were open.

It's 5:07 p.m. and supper is being held up briefly as the volunteers who are coming in to serve have not all yet arrived. There are about 25 people sitting around the multi – some at tables and some sitting on couches.

At 5:22 p.m., everyone is quietly seated at tables, ready to be served by the volunteers. The exception to the "quiet" is a crying baby in its mother's arms.

It's 8:10 p.m. on March 20. The multi purpose building is full of people getting ready to go to bed. People are lying on mattresses and couches all around the building.

There are 27 mattresses – about nine are vacant. Some people are also sitting on mattresses talking. Tonight the main office is still open and quite busy (whereas usually calls are handled by an answering service) because my text pager is not working. Consequently, we have someone in the office until 10 p.m. answering phones.

At 8:20 p.m., a young child is running around the multi. From my vantage point, I hear someone going to the CIPP office asking for a toothbrush. The driver comes in clutching eight dozen maple donuts. He asks for a key to the kitchen.

Minutes later, a woman who was here for some time on the CIPP Program but left and moved to Roswell says hello and thanks me for helping her out again. She is in Albuquerque for the night. She has come to bail out her husband, who is apparently in jail for public drunkenness.

She says "I miss this place; that's why I'm volunteering tonight." She doesn't tell me exactly what it is she's volunteering for.

At 8:55 p.m., a woman comes into the office to talk to the women's counselor, who is doing double duty answering the telephones. She had been written up in the log for being 'disruptive' during the previous night's church service. The woman is annoyed. She says that she wasn't at all disruptive, but had been laughing at a funny comment made by the pastor about "sex, drugs and rock 'n' roll."

I ask the chaplain (who is doubling up tonight as the driver) about the alleged comment. He says that he did say it and that it came out wrong, which is why it was funny. Instead of "Sex, drugs and rock 'n' roll," it came out as something like "Rock 'n' roll and drugs and eh, … sex." "It was funny the way I said it," the pastor says. More of that Joy Junction humor, I realize.

At 8:58 p.m., a child is crying loudly in the multi. The amount of noise has increased from a quiet, busy hum to just plain loud.

At 9:01 p.m., the lights should now be out, but evidently things are running a little late. Most people are now lying on their beds talking or reading. One man is sitting on his mattress fiddling with a roll of toilet paper and a woman is sitting on her mattress drearily combing out her hair.

At 9:04 p.m., the lights are turned out in the multi. (Lights are turned out in common areas at 9 p.m. and at 10 p.m. in private rooms). It's almost the end of another day at Joy Junction.

Appendix E
Who the Homeless Are (Interviews)
Interview Methodology

Questionnaires were given by me to 12 of the participants in Joy Junction's life skills program. The questions asked these individuals why and how they became homeless; how they interact with other people and live within the confines of the shelter and how they communicate the shelter's expectations to other people. (Individuals enrolled in this program are responsible for signing in and overseeing other homeless guests).

The respondents answered the questions wherever they chose within a day or so. It was essential that the subjects have the freedom to respond to the questionnaire without staff interference in order to retrieve their actual experiences.

The goal was to begin to identify some of the underlying reasons for homelessness from the vantage point of the homeless – as opposed to the media's.

I have reproduced the responses exactly as they were provided by the respondents. They were designed to invite narrative, and I used narrative in my analysis of the responses.

Respondent One – Interview

I became homeless because I was at one time working a full-time job. I had gotten very sick because I have ovarian cysts. Well, I ended up taking leave from my work and they fired me. I had enough money to pay for two months of rent and after that I couldn't afford it anymore. So I lost my apartment. My children and I moved in with some friends. My friend at that time said we could stay with her as long as I needed till I got back on my feet. Well, I had bought my own food and cleaned up around her house. Well a week later she kicked us out. This was Oct. 12, 2001. We went to stay with my parents for one night and the following day I found myself at Joy Junction.

(I live) quite well actually (within the confines of the shelter although) at first it was a shock to adjust to everything, but I eventually came to being okay with everything that goes on around me.

I myself have always been friendly with those around me. I generally try to treat people good if they treat me good.

Being on the CIPP program (shelter's life skills program, the Christ in Power Program) and working on the floor has taught me a lot. I have learned that in order to expect other people to follow the rules I must do it as well. I try to encourage those to see that being in a shelter and doing what is expected will help you grow in life to make things better in the "real" world. You have rules everywhere you go. If we didn't there would be a problem.

Respondent One – Analysis

Reading through this interview, I noticed but was not surprised by the number of times the respondent blamed other people. This theme was continued in her apparent belief that she was a victim of circumstance in that she writes that one day "I found myself at Joy Junction." There was no suggestion that she was responsible for any of the situations in which she found herself. Blaming other people for their misfortunes is something routinely done by the homeless.

On a more positive level, this lady realized that because it was her assignment to tell other people to follow the rules, it also meant that she had to do so.

Respondent Two – Interview

I am 35 years old. I became homeless due to my drug addictions. I have had several jobs and for periods of time do good, and then I just give up and begin using again.

People are very courteous in the shelter. I am grateful to have a second chance here at Joy Junction. People want to really better themselves here.

There are the people who attempt to use the system. Those are the ones who you want to stay away from.

The shelter life has brought me closer to my Lord and Savior.

There are a lot of people to interact with, at least 150 people at night. Most of the people here are positive especially after being on the CIPP program a couple of months.

There are people who want to complain about each and every rule there is, and it is funny they complain. Yet they need the shelter. People also tend to put on an (act) about how bad they are on the street or how much drugs they sell. But thankfully Joy Junction exists for those who really want and need it.

Respondent Two – Analysis

The respondent admitted responsibility for her actions, which is traditionally regarded as the first step in getting back on one's feet again. She also attributed a positive religious experience to the time she spent at Joy Junction, and provided an interesting insight about what she called people's exaggerated descriptions of their life on the street.

Respondent Three – Interview

(I became homeless because I was) smoking a lot of drugs and I didn't care what I did as long as I had my drugs. I had a lot of people using me like a dog. They moved in with me and my wife in my house but then it got out of hand and the cops were called up because of all the people that were over there and took a lot of people to jail because of all the pipes and drugs I had in my house; that is the reason why I am homeless now.

I would say people that live in a shelter means they are in trouble with their loved ones or they were living on the streets. I am glad that Joy Junction helps out people when they are in need of some help. I get along with a lot of people; a lot of people here just need someone to talk to because it's hard for some people to talk to others.

Some people like it here a lot because they can learn about Jesus Christ and how to help others. Some people say they don't like it because of all the gossip people say about them. I like the rules here at Joy Junction because it helps a lot of people here learn about respecting one another.

A lot of shelters around Albuquerque don't help families on there feet but I can tell you ever since I have been here it's helped me a lot. Especially when I am not doing drugs anymore, it has helped me with a lot of things, like making new friends with people that are homeless like I am.

I could call Joy Junction my home now because they have helped me out so much. Thank you so very much Joy Junction for the help that you have given to me.

Respondent Three – Analysis

The respondent admitted responsibility for his homelessness and was grateful for the help provided him at Joy Junction. His overall reaction to the shelter was positive. However, he felt that he was not able to call Joy Junction his home, maybe an important part of his getting back on his feet again, as I suspect that his formerly destructive lifestyle had destroyed positive relations with his family.

Respondent Four – Interview

My family became homeless because of an automobile accident. We were on our way to Albuquerque. The consequences of that accident depleted our resources and therefore here we are.

Being here is a blessing. Living within the boundaries that are set at Joy Junction can be restraining in that I constantly worry about crossing them unknowing. However they do (Unknowingly to many) help quite a bit in restraining our human nature. That being we are a self sabotaging lot.

Communication is simple for the most part. Be open and friendly yet decidedly guarded those you realize that defy the concept, try not to separate from. I find the best way to have questions answered is by deciding who would provide the full answer and go there. One sentence spoken can become an essay within minutes. The less said the better.

Respondent Four – Analysis

Although the respondent attributes his homelessness to an auto accident, there was obviously much more to it than that. For example, who was at fault, possible lack of insurance, why the "consequences of the accident" depleted the respondent's financial resources.

The respondent was grateful for Joy Junction and for the boundaries imposed at the shelter. He offered good advice about communicating with other guests staying at the shelter.

Respondent Five – Interview

We became homeless because the house where we were living was ruled to be unsafe due to the fact that a family member started a meth lab in our house. After that we had to leave so we ended up at a shelter.

I feel that people who live in a shelter live the same as other people do. At a shelter you have rules to live by that you may not have at your own home. Some of the rules include, no drinking, no staying out all night, no bring people over to stay with you, and you have to be at the shelter by 6:00 p.m. every night. So to me there's not that big of a difference. I treat everyone the same way no matter where they live. If I treat people bad just because they don't have their own home, then I am not a good person. It doesn't matter where you live, you should always treat people the same way.

At a shelter you're like a big family. Everyone eats together at a table and everyone has to clean so it's like one big house for a really big family. I let everyone know that shelter life can be helpful. When you come to a shelter they try and help you, and if you have a family they try and help them too. So that everyone who's there can try and get back on their feet. They help people when they can't help themselves.

At a shelter you go to church every Sunday, so that you can learn to put your trust in God. For some shelter life can be hard to get used to. If you're used to doing what you want when you want it will be hard. Living in a shelter will change your life in ways that may be hard to understand. I let people know that shelter life has helped my family and me. If it weren't for a shelter my family and me would not be able to stay together. I feel that shelter life is good for some people who need a little extra help in their life.

You may hear that shelters are dirty but that not always true. Shelters are cleaner than some houses.

At shelters you meet people that are just passing through and need a place to stay. And then there are people who have to live there because they have nowhere else to go. Shelters have family trying to stay together and people who have no home but want to find one. When you need help and you have no one to turn to you can always find a friend at a shelter. So when I am asked about a shelter and the life you live, I always say its helped my family and if you give it a try it can help yours.

Respondent Five – Analysis

While the respondent acknowledged the reason for her family's homelessness, he left unsaid the reason why he allowed a meth lab in her house. The explanation given almost seemed to imply that the meth lab was started in spite of her.

However, she accepted shelter standards and presented her opinion about how others should be treated as well as commenting that in her opinion, "Shelter life is good for some people who need a little extra help in their life." I noted that in presenting her comment in the third person it almost set her apart, as she did not appear to include herself as one of those who needed "a little extra help." The respondent expressed gratitude for the help given to her by Joy Junction.

Respondent Six – Interview

I became homeless six months ago. The beginning of my being homeless is when my marriage started to fade away. I looked for places to go. Finally I ended up here at Joy Junction.

After being here in the shelter for three months, I learned how to come closer with myself. I learned how to let go a lot my inner thoughts. I became closer to God.

Communication with other people, some was okay but I stayed away from the negative talk especially about others. When gossip was talked about (the) shelter (*sic*) my reply was we all should be thankful that we have a place to stay and to eat; a place that we could call home. My great expectation is to be able to better myself; and to be able to function on the outside as well as the inside.

It's sad to be homeless, but then again He can be helpful.

Respondent Six – Analysis

The respondent seemed to regard herself as being a victim of circumstance. However, she was grateful for what the shelter offered, encouraged others to be likewise and had a positive religious experience as well during her stay at Joy Junction.

Respondent Seven – Interview

I have experienced homelessness three times. The first time I had moved to Albuquerque from Nashville and had no one here but an abusive boyfriend. So I finally left him and stayed at the battered woman's shelter. This is where I met a lot of so called "friends." I got a job. One of the girls at the shelter got an apartment. This is when I was introduced to the heart of drugs (*sic*). The usage took over and eventually I was being evicted.

So I came to Joy Junction with my husband. I joined the CIPP program and my husband began working. I did not however complete the program, and left early. So the drugs returned for a while.

My husband's job transferred to Denver. There I found out I was pregnant again. So we cleaned up our act. Something inside me however was leading me back to Albuquerque. So I left a 2-bedroom apartment in Denver knowing I would be homeless and have to come to Joy Junction. My lease wasn't up until January and I had sub housing, but I chose to leave, but at this time in my life I know it was right decision to make. I am maturing as a Christian and my life is growing abundantly as is my walk with the Lord.

Living in a shelter environment is hard. I personally enjoy some of the structure when people become homeless and come into a shelter; they're looking for help. In order to genuinely help them they need structure. Men tend to have a harder time adjusting than women. They seem to go through an identity crisis at about the second week in a shelter. Working in the shelter

I've seen it in almost every couple. They're both stressed out and the men feel inadequate when that's not the case.

Interacting with people is a tricky situation. Some people don't want to talk; they want to wallow in pity. All you can do with these people is give them their space until their ready. Then be an open ear and a source of information.

They have rules to follow in shelters and the only way that I tell people rules are kindly. People don't want to be dictated. They already feel persecuted by society and there's a huge difference in asking someone to please do a chore and demanding that if it's not signed up for we won't eat. The response comes much faster to a smile than a blatant threat.

Respondent Seven – Analysis

The respondent admitted responsibility for her homelessness and equated her failure to complete Joy Junction's life skills program during her initial stay at the shelter with her return to drugs.

Getting pregnant was a sufficient motivation for her to stop using drugs. She equated living successfully with having a religious experience, offered her perspective on the reasons for homelessness and commented that rules work better when they are presented kindly. However, she also realized that effective communication is a difficult process.

Respondent Eight – Interview

In '95, my wife became involved with another man in my church. She has since married (same said man) and I am feeling myself (*sic*) for the last couple of years. I was a workaholic in marriage, working swings, and graveyard the last several years.

Homelessness for me has been a very conscious choice in a search for self. In '98, I came to Albuquerque and started working at Roses South Western paper, and from there to Ponderosa products. On the surface I was doing the right thing making money. Little by little art and music have been coming back into my life, as they were before marriage. Art in general is my gift for God.

In the fall of 2000, while going across the Civic Plaza downtown, I wrecked my mountain bike. My left collarbone was severely broken. It took two months before I could lift anything.

It was several months before I attempted any day labor. After my accident it did not occur to me that I was eligible for unemployment or any other assistance. Within two weeks after arriving in Albuquerque, I was aware of most of the homeless services in town. I went from social support services, to work for over one and one-half years and then back to the support system. I began to understand how the system in Albuquerque is perpetual.

You go from one line to another for food, for clothing, for servicing, to be acknowledging as a human being. You sometimes see people in line wanting attention with "I was here first or He cutting" and so you see people deny others at times to put themselves first.

I never felt part of the homeless crowd mentally, but that was, I believe a form of denial. I was in a habit. For a year I wondered what to do with myself.

In the fall of 2001, I came to Joy Junction, to see what it is about. It was immediately easy to be here because we have so many families here, and women. We have to keep everybody aware of Christian family values. Of course some people need more reminding than others, but what we have in place is better than any I've seen.

I was an overnighter five months ago. After two weeks of training on second shift, I was put on third shift on the floor. I lost a lot of sleep while in the multi working on the floor. Now in (room) B1-4, I rest enough and have space for my own life. I practice with flutes in the entryway of the multi for the acoustics and to stay in touch with my job. I know a few hundred homeless people.

My main experience here has been that all of these people look just like me. We are supposed to maintain a professional distance, and it can be hard when you think "there but for the Grace of God." So here with God's chosen people, my job and my life fit together as they never have before, seamless as an egg.

I was blessed with a passive nature, just letting most things go as they happen. There are very few people hard to relate to as far as I am concerned. My main focus of communication here is to find some common connection.

The shelter wants your children to not hear profanity is a way to ask a parent to stop using it. The operative word seems to be Awe as in with me also. If you separate yourself completely well then you are separate and as it is written, we may be the only Bible some people see.

Respondent Eight – Analysis

The respondent had a unique perspective on homelessness. "Homelessness for me has been a very conscious choice in a search for self." He did not seem to overtly admit responsibility for his homelessness. However, he felt that he had a handle on the social service system and provided a description from the point of view of a recipient of the number of steps involved in accessing the system.

It appeared that at Joy Junction he had found whatever it is for which he had been looking. "So here with God's chosen people my job and my life fit together as they never have before, seamless as an egg."

Respondent Nine – Interview

(My husband) and I went to live with my brother in October of 2001 because we couldn't find work in Oregon after we lost our jobs. Unfortunately, Denver isn't much better when someone has no money and no transportation. It was very difficult to find jobs. Eventually we both got jobs at the same place but then two weeks later my brother took Michael's check and kicked us both out. We used the last of our money to buy bus tickets to Albuquerque (Arizona was too expensive) once we were here another transient gave us the Joy Junction phone number and we called. That's how we ended up here.

Living in the shelter is very different from the outside. Mandatory church has been the hardest to get used to. However, I've always been an advocate of the rule. "If you live under someone else's roof, you obey their rules."

Being on the CNBC program has been a big help. It gives us a little extra money and in my case it helps me concentrate less on boredom (which results in me doing things that are against the rules) and in my husband's case, he has a job that he enjoys.

Interaction with the people here is no different than in a regular life. There are people we like and people we dislike.

It's very hard to make friends because people come and go so often. You'll never know who will be gone one month, one week or even on day after you meet them. That's why you befriend them while they're here and wish them luck when they're gone.

Volunteers are the most fun because when they're here, they seem to think that being homeless is some sort of contagious disease. At meals, when they serve trays, they are incredibly careful not to touch or talk to us. My husband and I have given ourselves the term "rabid bums" because that's what we get treated like at times.

Some volunteers are really nice, too. They laugh and joke with us, or tell us about themselves, and they truly seem to understand that the only (difference between) them and us is the turn of events in our lives. But even then, they know it isn't always the fault of the "residentially challenged" individual.

A lot of the people here, especially overnighters, hate being told what to do. As a floor person, my husband knows this more than I ever could. He gets all sorts of people in, and runs over the rules with each one. He reads the rule, gives and example of breaking the rule, and explains the consequences. If someone has a problem, he merely says, "Well, it's either follow the rules or sleep on the streets."

Respondent Nine – Analysis

Referring to herself as a transient, she advocated the motto that if you live under someone else's roof you should that obey their rules. However, since she and her husband were still evicted by her brother, it made me wonder if she observed that same standard while she and her husband were staying there. How compliant were they?

The respondent had a unique perspective on the volunteers with whom she interacted while staying at Joy Junction. While acknowledging that some volunteers were empathetic to the plight experienced by the homeless when staying at a shelter, others apparently though that "being homeless is some sort of contagious disease. At meals, when they serve trays, they are incredibly careful not to touch or talk to us. Michael and I have given ourselves the term 'rabid bums' because that's what we get treated like at times."

She realized that some guests staying at Joy Junction give all of the homeless a bad name and related that her husband encouraged everyone to accept the rules by saying, "Well, it's either follow the rules or sleep on the streets."

Respondent Ten – Interview

(My problems) all started back in 1995; my wife and I loved Bingo. We used to go at least three times a week. Then and later on down the road we started gambling on the machines, started off with the quarters machines, then we got greedy and hoping we would hit big one day. There was a time when we won five thousand dollars, and we thought that was our answer to our money problems. That's when we knew we had a problem with gambling, and lost everything, we landed coming to Joy Junction.

At first, it was very hard adjusting to the shelter, but we came to realize that the people at the shelter were normal people like us. But we started to realize that a lot of people at the shelter had the same problems or difficulties like any one else. So we believed that people at shelter were bad people. But we came to believe that they were normal as we are, but are in different problems. We came to respect them as human beings, and realize it could happen to any one. Which we never thought it could never happen to us because we looked at homeless people and thought how could that happen to any one.

And here we are in the same situation trying to make the best out of our situation, and never take any thing for granted and learned that is could happen to anybody. So we try to live each and every day to the best we can. By helping chores, that are available to keep busy and trying to set an example to others that not to loose hope. By talking to people that are in our situation making best of it. By listening to people and talking to other people letting them know that they're not alone, but there is light at the end of the tunnel and let them know that we have been there as of right now. And things have been getting better for us, and we will continue to have hope and there is help if you need it or want it, never loose hope. By letting every one know – the people we talk to – that it will get better by having faith and accepting faith in God that we were brought here for a reason that if we can at least try to except and take responsibility for actions that we got our selves into.

I believe that God has sent us here for a reason, but thank God this place is here to help and pick up the pieces and to take advantage of all of the program and if they are applied properly. We can all learn from all situations that we are in, and believe me it has helped us and to continue to help us. And others that intend different but after talking to few people, ask us how do we do it living here with all the rules.

We explain that if you need help to do the best they can and pray to all that some day things will get better each and every day. Keeping busy is the tool, of all our answers and have faith never to give up. Because God never gave up on each and every one, that it will get better, each and everyday to never lose hope. I feel that we are blessed for every day we're alive to talk about, and that we are not alone. And thank God has a mission for each, which one day we will find out and believe in him our Lord Christ.

Respondent Ten – Analysis

The respondent admitted responsibility for his homelessness and did not attempt to place the blame on anyone else. He wrote that staying at the shelter had given him an increased understanding of the reasons that people become homeless. The respondent showed a positive attitude, and tried to be an encouragement by setting a positive example for others staying at the shelter.

Respondent 11 – Interview

I became homeless by not managing my household, not setting priorities. I live in the confines of the shelter by taking it one day at a time. It's great to have your own (room?), but when you don't you just have to accept what you have. I feel I am blessed to be here at Joy Junction than to be on the streets. Sometimes I think maybe this is where God wants me to be for the time being.

I look at it that way and it helps me so much. I've join the CIPP program "Christ in Power," that's constructive to do while I am here in the shelter. I've also learned to pray earnestly for God's direction meditating on his word and courageously following the way indicated in the Bible often result in blessings beyond our expectation, but then we all should know leaning on God always leads to the best outcome in any situation.

I interact with other people very well. I get along with everyone here. You can't be friends with everyone but I love them all as God's children.

I've learned that I'm no better than anyone because anybody can become homeless. No matter what race or belief we have were all in the boat and guess what? God is the Boat. I communicate shelter expectations to others by telling them to be positive, respect, the rules, and try to use the shelter to better themselves. And let them know as it says in Proverbs 18:14, it is important to cultivate a good spirit.

Anything I can't help with I know to seek counsel before saying the wrong thing or making the wrong decision. Just remember God's word is a guide in all situations. The family is the oldest known human institution and that's what we are out here at the shelter. One big family, Joy Junction made me see its still possible for a family to be stable in a nurturing environment for all. We can actually help each other resolve a number of challenging situations as long as it agrees with Bible principle to preserve peace.

Respondent 11 – Analysis

This woman accepted responsibility for her homelessness and was grateful for the help that she found at Joy Junction. She said that she was helped by her strong religious faith, which also helped her love everyone else staying at Joy Junction "as God's children."

Respondent 12 – Interview

I became emotionally distraught after giving up my son. At that time I had pretty low self-esteem and losing him made me feel worthless; although it was my decision. Some women do not have a choice. I cannot imagine that choice being made for me.

I suffered from extreme depression. At that time I thought I was making coherent decisions (after he was gone mostly), but I was fearful, terrified and alone. I was emotionally wasted, empty. In a state of depression and shock, I did what I had to do to survive. And suffice to say, I was taken advantage of. I believe a combination of feeling worthless and trying to get help from compassionless people is what made me give up and become homeless; sad really.

(I live) quite well (within the confines of the shelter). I function well in a structured environment. Although I find some people and some situations frustrating at times, I know (because of my Lord, peace and patience) that it will eventually work out. I am adaptable. It also helps to be able to vent/discuss my feelings to a listening ear. I don't expect much, so when I think on things that really bother me, they're usually minor and deal able.

How do I interact with other people?

(I interact with other people) quite easily, mainly because of my inner peace. I dropped most of my control issues. I can't change ANYONE, but myself. Also bad company corrupts good character. After living for 37 years I've learned to spot people I just as soon avoid. I understand my boundaries. I am assertive, I am respectful, I am helpful, but refuse to be taken advantage of (this last one took many years to learn) I am free.

(I deal with others) directly (and) I pull no punches. Joy Junction is not condescending to me, consequently I will stick up for, defend this mission.

Respondent 12 – Analysis

The respondent appeared to blame her homelessness on the emotional distress she said she suffered after giving up her son. However, she did admit that giving up her child was her decision. She showed some ability to effectively self-analyze, realizing that the only person she could change was herself.

There was considerable strength in her last sentence. "(I deal with others) directly (and) I pull no punches. Joy Junction is not condescending to me, consequently I will stick up for, defend this mission."

Appendix F
The Homeless in Shelter Activity Logs

These incident logs, typically but not always negative, provide another "slice of life" at Joy Junction. As part of their duties, Joy Junction personnel and program participants record every incident that they feel needs to be known about or addressed by a shelter manager. These reports range from the police coming on property to allegations of drinking, drug use and such disagreements as "Gary got out of bed this morning and started arguing with Frank and then threatened to 'bash his face in.' I had to get Harold (a supervisor) to help break up the argument."

For reasons of confidentiality, only first names are used. My observations are contained in parentheses.

Log Records

2-24-02. 8:00 a.m.	Vanessa on duty training Kelly with keys and pager.
2-24-02. 9:40 a.m.	Per Harold floor people are not supposed to wake up CIPP people. (This is because part of the requirements of the CIPP program, which is geared toward getting people back on their feet again, is that they need to be able to wake up on their own initiative). The only rooms they are supposed to go into M room D-12 and D-7.
2-24-02. 9:45 a.m.	Nora and Robert slept in couch three where a fresh urine stain was found.
2-24-02. 11:40 a.m.	Seven couches were covered. Seven more couches need to be covered. One full roll of plastic was used. One more is needed.
2-24-02. 12:45 p.m.	All extra blankets were taken off the couches when the community service workers were putting plastic sheets on. It was noticed that some were personal.
2-24-02. 4:00 p.m.	Tiffany and Frank on duty with keys and pager.
2-24-02. 4:10 p.m.	David and Stephanie (C6-7-8) are stuck in Santa Rosa

tonight.

2-24-02. 5:45 p.m.   There are 10 lunches in the refrigerator please only eat one because the lunches for the morning are included, there are no more in the kitchen.

2-24-02. 10:05 p.m.   Sheriff's department on property to drop Monique off. Pastor Terry said no because of problem earlier this is her third time on alcohol list. (In order to ensure that people do receive some consequences for their actions, Joy Junction has what it calls an "alcohol list." An individual placed on that list for the first time will be banned from Joy Junction for a certain amount of time. If he or she keeps showing up at Joy Junction under the influence of alcohol, he or she will be banned for a progressively longer time for each infraction.) Sheriff took her back with him.

2-24-02. 10:10 p.m.   Couple had a Rottweiler in their truck, it got loose. They were informed the dog needed to be secured.

2-24-02. 11:02 p.m.   Attn: Harold we need copies of the security office logs please I could not find one tonight.

2-25-02.12:00 a.m.   Michael and Tom on duty with keys and pager.

2-25-02. 12:25 a.m.   Patrick came in drunk, and this was his third time on the alcohol list. Driver took him to People for Jesus church on 5600 Central SW.

2-25-02. 12:50 a.m.   Rita called in as Lois and the van driver did not pick her up as she is on the not welcome list.

2-25-02. 2:15 a.m.   Greg called several times after hours asking about his wife Tonya, He was told that no information could be given over the phone about residents.

2-25-02. 5:10 a.m.   Overnighters Rose and Billie as well as Donna went to St. Martin's on the 4:30 run instead of Labor Express and Francisca, D-7 B-4 has not been going to labor express either. She meets up with some man and walks toward Central. (There are consequences for actions listed here. This report will be read by shelter management and appropriate steps will be taken to

	correct the situation. The corrective action will usually start with a verbal warning, and if that fails to produce a change in behavior, an individual will probably be banned from the shelter for a certain period of time.)
2-25-02. 6:00 a.m.	There was a confrontation between overnighters Doug and Jessie. They were yelling in each other's faces, slapping and pushing the two were separated and told to stay away from each other. This is the second confrontation in the past week. (Action will be taken once a member of management is made aware of this.)
2-25-02. 7:00 a.m.	We got a bag with 36 rolls of "TP" from the linen closet.
2-25-02. 7:25 a.m.	Sasha (C-14) is again walking around dressed inappropriately per Joy Junction dress code. (Joy Junction's dress code requires that undergarments be worn and that midriffs, etc, are not shown.) She has been told by floor staff to cover her top and she gets an attitude. She was seen strutting and dancing around on the patio. This needs to be addressed. Also note, their son Brandon is going in the mornings to sell papers instead of going to school.
2-25-02. 8:00 a.m.	Amy and Vanessa on duty with keys and pager.
2-25-02. 9:00 a.m.	Amy went to ER.
2-25-02. 12:00 p.m.	Tonya D7, B7 is in the hospital won't be in to work. Will call when they release her.
2-25-02. 1:00 p.m.	Sheriffs on property, talking to Adrian.
2-25-02. 1:20 p.m.	Sheriffs left property, looking for old resident.
2-25-02. 2:05 p.m.	Nelson, Irene SC-2 needs to leave on the 6:45 a.m. van to downtown.
2-25-02. 2:30 p.m.	Tom H. on duty with keys and pager per Jeremy.
2-25-02. 3:10 p.m.	Cory and another person walked across field towards streets informed that it is Mathew and Sasha's son who walked across field. (This was another violation of shelter policy. Joy Junction's neighbors to the immediate north have been very concerned that walking

across the fields belonging to the shelter places the homeless in much too close proximity to their houses and they have asked us to ensure that this is curtailed.)

2-25-02. 3:30 p.m. Sherry C-5 will be admitted into the hospital tomorrow and won't be back for two days.

2-25-02. 3:30 p.m. Tom gives keys and pager back to Vanessa and clocks out.

2-25-02. 4:00 p.m. Stacy and Frank on duty with key and pager.

2-25-02. 7:45 p.m. Amy's kids are with Vanessa Barracks II Room 3. Amy still at hospital.

2-25-02. 10:00 p.m. Annie is on the not welcome list for 3 months. She was told by morning shift that we would sign her up for 30 days. Per Harold she was given a ride back to town.

2-25-02. 10:00 p.m. Stephanie and Debra Davies got mad about the sleeping arrangements & they went off on us (Stacy and Harold) (These are two women who apparently want to sleep in the same bed.) Per Harold they are on not welcome list. They both then asked for a ride back to town. Attn: Please Remind Harold to talk to Jeremy R. about how long to keep them on the not welcome list tomorrow.

2-25-02. 10:45 p.m. Shawna (D-12 Bed 4) and Regina (D-12 R1) got into an argument. Regina was moved to the multi. C-7 for the night. Have first shift O.K. it with Eric or Harold to move Regina (D-12 R1) to the multi for the rest of her stay.

2-25-02. 11:00 p.m. There are three bags in the CIPP office that belong to Betty who is blind. She is on SC-21 by the woman's restroom.

2-26-02. 12:00 a.m. Michael and Chris on duty with keys and pager.

2-26-02. 3:15 a.m. On 2-25-02 overnighter Nora signed out a whole roll of toilet paper.

2-26-02. 3:25 a.m. Note: The dumpster for the multi was left open.

2-26-02. 3:50 a.m. There was no log sheet for the time in and out for office

	security. Still not being in this habit yet, I failed to notice the lack of paperwork and will make a point to keep on top of it (Acknowledgement of responsibility.)
2-26-02. 6:05 a.m.	We had to confirm Terence of E-2, had a trip to town. Michael called Terry.
2-26-02. 8:00 a.m.	Vanessa on duty with keys and pager.
2-26-02. 1:30 p.m.	Per Harold we need to get mattress to replace lost mattress from donation trailer. They need to be dry and covered in plastic. (This is a Bernalillo County Environmental Health Department requirement. Plastic covering helps prevent bed bugs and anything similar crawling off one resident to another and also makes the mattresses easier to wash down. It also helps prevent mice getting into the mattresses. If the mattresses are not dry, it may indicate a presence of urine.)
2-26-02. 2:30 p.m.	Attn: second shift: Can you please move Stephan and Michelle M2, Martin and Patricia M3 & 4 and Jewel M1 to couches, I (Vanessa) have a family that needs to be placed.
2-26-02. 3:00 p.m.	Per Harold: New residents are not to be on couches unless they have a child under 2.
2-26-02. 3:30 p.m.	Dorm room 9 needs to be cleaned out really bad.
2-26-02. 5:45 p.m.	Ambulance called for Thomas (Barracks 1 Room 2) He had a heart attack. Ambulance came and took Tom and Edna to Lovelace Cardiac unit for treatment and for exam.
2-26-02. 6:10 p.m.	Tiffany and Stacy were on duty at 4:00 p.m.
2-26-02. 6:11 p.m.	Harold wanted it logged that Karen (D7, B10) was interfering when Thomas collapsed. Karen said she was a qualified EMT and began performing her work.
2-26-02. 6:35 p.m.	Harold asked me to log that Karen (D7, B10) was butting in again with Kelly (D7 B9). Kelly came to let Harold know she's having blood sugar problems and Karen came and put her "professional" opinion in. (Actions like those shown by Karen can be too common

around a shelter. Homeless people tend to naturally gravitate toward the emergency services when they come. Sometimes there are guests who claim that they are medically qualified. Unless they can produce proof of their qualifications, we always decline their services.)

2-26-02. 6:35 p.m.   Kerry (SMC 20) was seen going toward the warehouse. Stacy (floor) went to get him. He was getting some stuffed animals that were in the trash, out to give to the kids.

2-26-02. 6:40 p.m.   I Stacy explained to Kerry (SMC-20) that he could not be back by the warehouse after they close warehouse or unless he was helping out in the warehouse. Kerry (SMC-20) said he did not know and that he would not do it again. I told Harold about it he said to log it.

2-26-02. 7:35 p.m.   7:15 p.m. Lawrence back on property.

2-26-02. 7:36 p.m.   Patricia and Renee came onto property; they left property via van because they did not want to attend church. (As a faith-based ministry, mandatory attendance at church services is an integral part of what Joy Junction does. It goes to the very core of our reason for existence. While many in the community still think of us as being an "agency," we refer to ourselves as a faith-based ministry. As a ministry that elects not to receive any government funding of any type, we are permitted to mandate church attendance.) Close to time of church, they called answering service for a pick-up. Harold called Eric and Eric said not to pick them up. Harold wants it logged that they be put on not welcome list for 30 days *for their little stunt*. (An interesting choice of words by our floor program participant personnel, which showed quite a lot of cynicism.)

2-26-02. 7:44 p.m.   I utilized the space in d-9 to put a family of 5 in for tonight. Their names are Cheryl and Ricky. They need to be assigned to a permanent couch tomorrow.

2-26-02. 7:45 p.m.   We need bleach for the CIPP office.

2-26-02. 7:46 p.m. We need to have Tom (B1, R2) fill out a medical emergency form. I put his name on one and put it in the black folder.

2-26-02. 7:52 p.m. William and Diane checked out because they could not get a curfew extension to go sit at the hospital with Tom and Edna.

2-26-02. 9:19 p.m. Gary is on SC 25. He is here on medical. He turned in his medical papers they are in the black folder.

2-26-02. 9:30 p.m. Shawna back on property.

2-26-02. 10:20 p.m. Per Harold first shift needs to have Rae get the mats out of storage trailer and bring them back to the multi. So first shift can put plastic on them and on any couch that has a mat but not plastic cover. Eric is getting the plastic so check with Eric for the plastic when he comes in.

2-26-02. 10:35 p.m. These couches are already covered (the rest need to be covered) C3, C4, C6, C7, C8, C12, C13.

2-26-02. 10:40 p.m. Received a page after lights out for Betty to call her husband at the hospital Room 105 764-8870.

2-26-02. 10:50 p.m. The food in the gray bags in the fridge belongs to Brown, Rose and overnighter.

2-27-02. 12:00 a.m. Michael, Chris and Tom on duty with keys and pager.

2-27-02. 1:50 a.m. Edna BI-2 returned from Lovelace on Gibson, where Tom was checked in for heart attack.

2-27-02. 1:40 a.m. Brandon is on a SM in the doorway of the classroom by his parents who are Matthew and Sasha on G 14. Brandon is blocking a fire exit where he is. We need Harold's help here. (The individuals we call our "floor people" are homeless guests staying at the shelter who are members of our life-skills program, CIPP. They oversee the registration of residents and a number of other duties. However, if there is an issue where another resident will not obey them, the floor people have instructions to write the issue up in the log, and mark it for the attention of a staff manager.)

2-27-02. 2:00 a.m.   Attention: second shift: We need the dumpster lids closed at all times.

2-27-02. 2:20 a.m.   The smell of cigarette smoke was coming heavily from Kathy's D-4 room. (Illicit smoking is a continuing problem where guests staying at the shelter have earned a private room. We have smoke and heat detectors in every room of all of our buildings.)

2-27-02. 2:20 a.m.   David, D-6, was taken to UNM to have his ear checked out. He said his left ear was causing him pain and he could not hear from it. It is possibly infected since we have three floor persons we will cover security until he returns or 5 a.m.

2-27-02. 2:30 a.m.   Three soda cans were found empty surrounding Mathew and Sasha's couch C-14 and an empty bag of candy and many candy wrappers were found next to David and Edna's Mat M-5. (Guests staying at the shelter are not permitted to keep food in the multi area, because it draws mice. Other guests noticing the mice often make a call to the County Health Department, who unexpectedly come to the shelter very concerned about Joy Junction's "mice" infestation.)

2-27-02. 2:50 a.m.   Tom has volunteered to take David's security round since David is at UNM.

2-27-02. 3:35 a.m.   A can of "Steele Reserve" was found in the woman's bathroom trash.

2-27-02. 3:40 a.m.   Ruth M-4, got up and went and laid down on C-8. When told she had to go back to her assigned bed she got angry and called me a bitch. MDR (There is much hostility and a fairly routine unwillingness to obey rules. Many times it was attitudes like this that resulted in people becoming homeless in the first place.)

2-27-02. 5:05 a.m.   David, D-6, back on property with med. papers exempting him from work through 2-28.

2-27-02. 5:15 a.m.   Tito (C-15) was seen walking toward the front the multi building (east side), he stated he was supposed to meet

	a friend, I told him he could not be outside till 5:30 a.m. and to go back indoors.

2-27-02. 5:30 a.m.   There was a white pick-up truck that dropped off "T's" husband and "T" and husband were seen entering room, Pastor Terry was called because the visitor didn't sign in, and things looked suspicious. Pastor Terry responded and asked visitor to leave, and explained the rules to both of them they did not appear under the influence.

2-27-0. 7:00 a.m.   Tina, overnighter on C-6 with Ismael refused at first to move from couch to allow me to make the cover. Once she did move it was with a lot of profanity mainly the F-word (This is an example of more hostility.)

2-27-02.7:15 p.m.   It was reported that for the last two mornings overnighter Mary has been going over to the dorm to use the restroom and coincidentally some minor possessions have turned up missing. Also two overnighters were put in D-7 for the night on beds 12 and 14. The person on 12 has no paperwork that we can find. Both she and Purcell were arguing with the ladies in D-7, especially Francisca, D-7 B-4, who was threatened with bodily harm (More hostility.) The two ladies also smelled heavily of alcohol to the residents of D-7, neither were put on the alcohol list. Lee has now been added.

2-27-02. 8:00 a.m.   Amy and Vanessa on duty training Kelly with keys and pager.

2-27-02. 8:45 a.m.   Pastor Terry informed Devore, Leonard SMC-18 that he cannot leave property with out approval from staff. (This man has serious medical problems.)

2-27-02. 9:30 a.m.   This AM Amy was informed there was a fight in D-12. Amy got me (Vanessa) and we went over. We were then informed that per Harold second shift had warned them that if there was any more fighting going on they were going to be asked to leave because the floor people are too busy to have to referee all the time.

Apparently, this time the argument was again between Regina (D-12 B1) and Shawna (D-12 B4). Vanessa informed them that this has to stop. We were informed by Shawna (D-12 B4) that she was going to speak with Rae. today. (While there is hostility like this going on\frequently at Joy Junction, there could be more. The environment is quite tense, because so many people from such a variety of backgrounds are suffering from and dealing with many life-controlling problems. In addition, they are homeless and living in close quarters.)

2-27-02. 11:00 a.m.   Per Rae. B She wants to see Regina (D12 B1) and Shawna (D-12 B4) in her office together when they are both on property. She requests that a floor person be present at that time in her office.

2-27-02. 11:00 a.m.   Fire Department here on property for a controlled burn in the field. Emergency page sent out.

2-27-02. 11:15 a.m.   Matthew and Sasha (C-14) and Rachelle (MM7) were caught eating at the table between mealtime and they were informed by Kelly to please take their food outside. Mathew proceeded to have an attitude about it and said "Well I see the rules change here on a daily basis."

2-27-02. 3:15 p.m.   "T" telephoned office to state she will be late – she will be here around 11:00 p.m. per Frances (in office).

2-27-02. 4:00 p.m.   Stacy, Tiffany and Frank on duty with keys and pager.

2-27-02. 6:45 p.m.   Edna and David are on the not welcome list for 3 months per Eric S. (manager) for yelling at other residents and manager. (This is an example of more hostility.)

2-27-02. 7:55 p.m.   Emergency vehicles here for Ricky. He had two seizures so they are transporting him to UNMH ER.

2-27-02. 11:30 p.m.   Tammy needs to go to UNMH.

2-28-02. 12:15 a.m.   Per Eric Shawna (D12 B4) and Morgan, Regina (D-12 B1) are to be moved back to the multi if they fight with one another one more time.

2-28-02. 12:20 a.m.   "T's" (D5 B1) did not come back tonight she had a

	curfew extension till 11:00 p.m. but never came in or called.
2-28-02. 12:06 a.m.	Tom and Chris on duty with keys and pager.
2-28-02. 12:30 a.m.	"T's" (D5 B1) back on property.
2-28-02. 1:00 a.m.	The vans were left with one-quarter tank of gas. Please leave one with enough gas for the shift.
2-28-02. 2:30 a.m.	We need a lock on the donation truck by the main office.
2-28-02. 3:05 a.m.	Van driver had to switch to new van (#4) to have enough gas.
2-28-02. 4:00 a.m.	Attention second shift floor and security please check dumpster and keep it closed.
2-28-02. 4:05 a.m.	Short form marked as S.F. has either two single females named Ivasco over 18, or a couple listed as single residing in D-9.
2-28-02. 4:08 a.m.	Diane over night on C-4 has a child with no name or age.
2-28-02. 4:10 a.m.	Betty is signed up as single female on SC-21 for 2-27-02 yet she is with a man with a different name on C-5.
2-28-02. 8:00 a.m.	Amy on duty and training Kathleen with keys and pager.
2-28-02. 10:00 a.m.	Susan (SM 7) yelled at Betty (D7 B13) and myself (Amy) about going in there and using the women's restroom she was standing there washing her feet and was fully clothed, there was no reason for her to not let anyone else in the restroom. She has a bad attitude and does not want to listen to any of the floor people. Can someone from management please have a talk with her. (An unwillingness to listen to rules and be reasonable are quite common characteristics for some of the guests who stay at Joy Junction and many of the other homeless shelters available nationwide.)
2-28-02. 1:30 p.m.	Ambulance called for David (D-6) to go to UNMH ER.
2-28-02. 1:45 p.m.	Ambulance left property to take David and Mindy to UNMH ER.

2-28-02. 1:46 p.m.   David (D6) was taken to UNMH ER for a possible allergic reaction to his medicine, abdominal pain, headache, blurred vision, stiff neck as well.

2-28-02. 2:00 p.m.   Attention all shifts: If the intercom is not working please go into the attic and check to see if the green light is on the amplifier. The amplifier is located on top of where the phone lines are to the right of the attic stairs.

2-28-02. 2:05 p.m.   Susan (M-7) is constantly leaving her dirty (snotted on) tissues everywhere. In the women's restroom and outside. She was caught once by Michael (D-2) when she threw her tissue in the bush outside. I have approached her about this already and she gets argumentative and rude and claims she can't recall herself doing so. (This is an example of more bad attitudes.)

2-28-02. 2:20 p.m.   David and Mindy (D-6) were not able to go to UNMH ER because it was to full so the ambulance transported them to St. Joseph's Hospital downtown, and it is OK'd by Harold E. for the van driver to pick them up when they call.

2-28-02. 3:15 p.m.   Locker (C-7) was emptied today and the personal items are in the CIPP office and are to be given to Harold E. tomorrow if they don't come back for them tonight. AGT.

2-28-02. 3:45 p.m.   I (Amy) and (Kelly) emptied out locker (C-7). The personal items went into the CIPP office and the rest went into a garbage bag to be taken to the dumpster. Matthew (C-14) was going to take the items to the dumpster when out of the multi patio he gave the bag of belongings to another new resident Daniel, (No bed assignment yet) who was going through it and taking what he wanted. I told Matthew he wasn't allowed to keep that stuff and it needs to go to the dumpster immediately. He was upset about that factor, but said he would do so. I (Amy) am going to talk with Matthew

(C-14) about the incident. Mathew said he did in fact go and throw it in the dumpster, Frank was a witness to this, and Daniel took it out of the dumpster for his own usage.

2-28-02. 4:00 p.m.	Stacy and Frank on duty with keys and with pager.
2-28-02. 9:15 p.m.	Deborah (D-7 B-2) says her last night will be Sunday, she got a place and is moving out on Monday.
2-28-02. 9:30 p.m.	Sandra (D-8) dorm parent and Stacy (D-8) dorm parent and Kathleen (D-7 B-9) cleaned out lockers 12 and 14 in D-7 the stuff is in the linen room on the stage.
2-28-02. 9:45 p.m.	Per Eric S. He wants floor staff to call at 3:30 a.m. as he is coming to cook breakfast.

Appendix G
Analysis of Shelter Log Data

There were a variety of issues that I saw from my ethnographic observation, interviews and incident logs that appeared to be apparent reasons for homelessness. They included a) mental illness, b) overt hostility, c) drug and alcohol abuse, d) refusal to obey rules and e) an unwillingness to accept responsibility for one's actions.

Many of the individuals observed and interviewed did not appear to act in ways that would be conducive to their obtaining and keeping jobs or being able to rent a place to stay. Consequently, their homelessness was more than just lacking a place to stay. The condition of their homelessness was a result (albeit indirect) of the actions mentioned above.

References

Alford, K. L. (1997). *The impact of social learning theory in an entertainment-education radio soap opera.* Unpublished master's thesis, University of Pennsylvania.

Anastasio, P. A., Rose K. C. and Chapman J. (1999). Can the media create public opinion? A social identity approach. *Current Directions in Psychological Science, 8,* 152–155.

Bandura, A. (1977). *Social learning theory.* Englewood Cliffs, NJ: Prentice-Hall.

Buck and Toro, P. A. (2002). Public opinion on homelessness in the United States and other developed nations. Retrieved Nov. 28, 2005, from http://66.102.7.104/search?q=cache:RB8E_eQygC8J:sun.science.wayne .edu/~ptoro/encych8.pdf+%22buck+and+toro%22&hl=en&ie=UTF-8

Caton, C. L. M. (1990). *Homeless in America.* New York: Oxford University Press.

Center for Media and Public Affairs. (1990). *Media coverage of the homeless 1986–1989.* Washington, D.C.: Author.

Christian, J. (1994). *Powerless of the poor: Toward an alternative kingdom of God based paradigm of response.* Unpublished dissertation, Fuller Theological Seminary, Pasadena, CA.

Christian, J. (1998). A different way to look at poverty. In *Body and soul.* London: World Vision UK.

Christian, J. (1999). *God of the empty handed: Poverty, power and the kingdom of God.* Monrovia, CA World Vision.

Cohen, B. (1963). *The press and foreign policy.* Princeton, NJ: Princeton University Press.

Coombs, P. H. and Ahmed, M. (1974). *Attacking rural poverty: How non-formal education can help.* Baltimore: Johns Hopkins University Press.

Dearing, J. W. and Rogers, E. (1996). *Agenda-setting.* Thousand Oaks: Sage Publications.

Fadul, A. (1993). *Serial fiction in TV: The Latin American telenovelas.* San Paulo Brazil: University of San Paulo.

Foley, G. (1999). *Learning in social action: A guide to understanding informal education.* London and New York: Zed Books.

Freedom Forum. (1997). Sources journalists use. Retrieved May 4, 2005, from www.freedomforum.org/fac/publicat/gap/5first.html).

Glaser, B. G. and Strauss, A. L. (1967). *Discovery of grounded theory: Strategy for qualitative research.* New York: de Gruyter.

Glaser, B. G. and Corbin, J. (1998). *Basics of qualitative research: Techniques and procedures for developing grounded theory.* Thousand Oaks, CA: Sage Publications.

Harris, R. J. (2004). *A cognitive psychology of mass communication.* Mahwah, NJ: Lawrence Erlbaum.

Hartman, P. and Husband, C. (1974). *Racism of the mass media.* London: Davis-Pointer.

Hewitt, C. (1996). Estimating the number of homeless: Media misrepresentation of an urban problem. *Journal of Urban Affairs*, 23–45.

Hilbert, P. G. (1989). The flaw of the excluded middle. *Missiology*, 10 (1), 35–47.

Katz, W. A. (1992). *Magazines for libraries.* New York: Bowker.

Kinnick, K. N. (1994). *Compassion fatigue: An investigation of audience burnout toward social problems.* Unpublished dissertation, University of Pennsylvania.

Kinsey, D. C. and Bing, J. W. (1978). *Non-formal education.* Massachusetts: Center for International Education.

La Belle, T. J. (1976). *Non-formal education and social change in Latin America.* Los Angeles: UCLA Latin America Publications.

La Belle, T. J. (1986). *Non-formal education in Latin America and the Caribbean.* Westport, CT: Praeger.

Lawrence, S. (February 24 – March 3, 2004). Body Bag Journalism. *Croswinds Weekly.*

Lichter, S. R. and Rothman, S. and Lichter, L. S. (1986). *The media elite: America's new powerbrokers.* Bethesda, MD: Adler & Adler.

Liebow, E. (1993). Tell them who I am: The lives of homeless women. New York: Penguin Books.

MacLean, P. D. (1973). *A triune concept of the brain and behavior.* Toronto: University of Toronto Press.

Maddoux, M. (1990). *Free speech or propaganda: How the media distorts the truth.* Nashville, TN: Thomas Nelson.

McCombs, M. (1994). News influences on our picture of the world. In J. Bryant and D. Zillmann (Eds.), *Media effects: Advances in theory and research.* Hillsdale, NJ: Lawrence Erlbaum.

McCombs, M. E. and Shaw, D. L. (1972). The agenda-setting function of mass media. In: *Public Opinion Quarterly,* 36, 176–187.

McNulty, B. R. (1992). *Homeless and hopeless: Resignation in news media constructions of homelessness as a social problem.* Unpublished dissertation, University of Pennsylvania.

Min, E. (1999). *Reading the homeless: The media's image of homeless culture.* Westport, CT: Praeger.

Myers, Bryant L. (1999). *Walking with the poor.* Maryknoll, NY: Orbis Books.

Nariman, H. N. (1993). *Soap operas for social change: Toward a methodology for entertainment-education television.* Westport, CT: Praeger.

Newcomb, H. (1974). *TV: The most popular art.* Garden City, NY: Anchor Press.

Olasky, M. (1991). *Central ideas in the development of American journalism: A narrative history.* Mahwah, NJ: Lawrence Erlbaum.

Olasky, M. (1992). *The tragedy of American compassion.* Washington, DC: Regnery Publishing.

Paul, G. (2004). *God in the alley.* Colorado Springs, CO: Shaw.

Pew Research Center for the People and the Press. (2002, June 9). Public's news habits little changed by September 11: Americans lack background to follow international news. Retrieved May 4, 2005, from http://people-press.org/reports/display.php3?ReportID=156

Pew Research Center for the People and the Press. (2004, November 11). Voters liked campaign 2004, but too much 'mud-slinging,' moral values: How important? Retrieved May 4, 2005, from http://people-press.org/reports/display.php3?ReportID=233.

Piotrow, P. T. (1997). *Health communication.* Westport, CT: Praeger.

Powter, J. G. (1991). *Mass communication of otherness and identification: An examination of the portrayal of homeless people in network television news.* Unpublished Doctoral Dissertation, University of Southern California.

Rivers, W., Schramm, W., and Christians, C. (1980). *Responsibility in mass communications* (rev. ed.). New York: Harper & Row.

Sanchez-Ruiz, Enrique E. (1983). *Capital accumulation: The state and television as informal education.* Unpublished Dissertation, University of Stanford.

Singhal, A. and Rogers, E. (1999). *Entertainment-education: A communication strategy for social change.* Mahwah, NJ: Lawrence Erlbaum.

Whang, I. S. (1993). *A structuralistic narrative analysis of television evening news coverage of the homeless, 1985–1991.* Unpublished dissertation, Ohio State University.

Index

About the Author

Jeremy Reynalds holds a Ph.D. in intercultural education from Biola University in Los Angeles and a master's degree in communication from the University of New Mexico.

Dr. Reynalds is the founder and executive director of Joy Junction, New Mexico's largest emergency homeless shelter, which provides food, shelter, clothing and a faith-based approach to recovery and returning to mainstream society from living on the periphery.

He was a contributor to Reading the Homeless (Praeger, 1999) with a chapter entitled "Informing and Educating the Media — A Hopeful Perspective on the Media and the Homeless." Dr. Reynalds is also the author of War of the Web (World Ahead Publishing, 2006) in which he analyzes the covert world of online terrorist activity.